The Art of Change Management

IMPLEMENTING CHANGE FROM THE TOP

by **PERCY AGRERAS DASTUR** Ph.D.

EMBASSY BOOKS
www.embassybooks.in

The Art of CHANGE MANAGEMENT

© Percy Dastur 2010
First Published in India: 2010

Published by:
EMBASSY BOOK DISTRIBUTORS
120, Great Western Building,
Maharashtra Chamber of Commerce Lane,
Fort, Mumbai-400 023, (India)
Tel : (+91-22) 22819546 / 32967415
email : embassy@vsnl.com
Website: www.embassybooks.in

All rights reserved. No part of this book may be used or reproduced in any manner whatsoever without written permission from the publishers, except in the case of brief quotations embodied In articles and reviews.

ISBN 13: 978-93-80227-60-3

Book and Cover Design: Namrata Chattaraj.
e-mail: namzie@gmail.com

Printed and Bound in India by
M/s. Repro India Ltd., Mumbai

The Art of Change Management

*This book is dedicated to my Parents
Agreras and Sanober Dastur*

Only the wisest and stupidest of men never change.

~ Confucius ~

Everybody has accepted by now that change is unavoidable. But that still implies that change is like death and taxes - it should be postponed as long as possible and no change would be vastly preferable. But in a period of upheaval, such as the one we are living in, change is the norm.

~ Peter Drucker ~

Management Challenges for the 21st Century

Change is the law of life and those who look only to the past or present are certain to miss the future.

~ John F. Kennedy ~

CONTENTS

Acknowledgements .... *xi*
Introduction .... *xiii*

CHAPTER 1: INTRODUCTION TO CHANGE

Organisational Change: What is it? *02*
Types of Organisational Change *04*
The Change Drivers *09*
Broad Context for Organisational Change and Development *12*
Change and the Role of a Leader *18*

CHAPTER 2: THE CHANGE PROCESS

Phases of The Change Process *22*
Phase I: Addressing Clarifications related to Roles and
Expectations for Change Process *24*
Phase II: Identifying Priorities of Change *27*
Phase III: Planning the Organisational Development
Activities to address the identified priorities *29*
Phase IV: Change Management & Evaluation *36*

CHAPTER 3: RESISTANCE TO CHANGE

Resistance to Organisational Change Initiatives *42*
Reactions to Change *44*
Reasons for an Organisational failure to overcome
resistance to Change *49*
Best Practices to Overcome Resistance to Change *54*
Skills & Competencies required to Overcome Resistance to Change ... *59*
Approach to Managing Organisational Change *62*

CHAPTER 4: ROLE OF TOP MANAGEMENT IN HANDLING CHANGE

Key Roles during Change Management	73
The Role of Top Management	75
Participation of Board of Directors in the Process of Change	83
The importance of playing Facilitator, Coach and Trainer	86
Managing Change Successfully – How Can CEOs achieve this?	87

CHAPTER 5: TYPES OF MANAGEMENT STRATEGIES IN HANDLING CHANGE

Change Management Strategies	99
Empirical – Rational Strategy	100
Normative – Reeducative Strategy	103
Power – Coercive Strategy	109
Environmental – Adaptive Strategy	113
How do I select the right Strategy?	117

CHAPTER 6: ROLE OF TOP MANAGEMENT IN COMMUNICATING ORGANISATIONAL CHANGE

Significance of Communicating Change	121
Factors Involved in Communicating Change	122
Communicating Change: Kotter's Perspective	125
Role of Team Leaders in each Business Division	127
Communicating Organisational Change at the Local Level	131
Establishing Performance Benchmarks and Rewarding Performance	133
Face to Face Performance Reviews	134
Communication: A concluding note	135

CHAPTER 7: ROLE OF THE CEO IN SUCCESSFUL ORGANISATIONAL CHANGE

Painting a Powerful Vision *141*

Inspiring Change *144*

Gathering Political Support *148*

Managing Transition *149*

Sustaining the Energy *151*

CHAPTER 8: ATTRIBUTES OF CEO AND ORGANISATIONAL CHANGE

CEO Tenure and Attitude towards Change *161*

CEO Experiential Attributes and Organisational Change *164*

CEO Origin, Strategic Change and Firm Performance *168*

CEO Functional Background and Diversity and Organisational Change *173*

CEO Ego Development Stages and Organisational Change *176*

Analogies between Personal and Organisational Development Stages *180*

CHAPTER 9: ROLE OF THE CEO IN SUCCESSION PLANNING

What is SPM? *186*

Why is Succession Planning essential? *187*

The Board and the CEO in SPM *194*

The CEO and SPM *199*

CHAPTER 10: ABLE CEOs LEADING THE ORGANISATIONAL CHANGE

What can we learn from them? *211*

Jack Welch: speed, simplicity, self confidence *224*

Michael Dell: the mind that made Dell *228*

CHAPTER 11: CONCLUSION *234*

LIST OF FIGURES   Page

Figure 1.1: Classification of Organisational Change   5

Figure 1.2: Types of Organisational Change   8

Figure 1.3: Approaches to Change   17

Figure 2.1: Phases in the Change process   23

Figure 2.2: Different Types of Client categories   24

Figure 3.1: Resistance to Change   41

Figure 3.2: Square Wheels by Dr. Simmerman   53

Figure 3.3: Approaches to Effective Change Management   64

Figure 4.1: Key Roles in Change Management   73

Figure 5.1: Change Management Strategies   100

Figure 5.2: Phases in the Implementation of Normative-Reeducative Strategy   105

Figure 6.1: Factors involved in communicating Change   122

Figure 6.2: Kotter's building blocks for a powerful Change communication   125

Figure 6.3: A simple skeletal framework for effectively coordinating Change   128

Figure 6.4: Activities to be performed by core group   129

Figure 7.1: Phases of Change   138

Figure 7.2: CEO's role in successful Organisational Change   141

Figure 8.1: U-shaped relationship of Strategic Change with firm performance   170

Figure 9.1 – Types of Succession Plans   193

Acknowledgment

The Art of Change Management has been a very special project for me as it is a culmination of various experiences accumulated over a period of time.

I am deeply grateful to my parents, sister, wife and children whose continuous support and encouragement has made this book happen. It is they who are my guiding light all the way.

I also wish to thank my mentor Dr. Chandran Dinesh whose guidance has encouraged me to strive to achieve excellence.

Finally a very special mention needs to be made for my friend, Dr. Sandeep Ramakant Sawant, to whom I credit the reason for me to write this book.

Introduction

"Men make history, and not the other way around. In periods where there is no leadership, society stands still. Progress occurs when courageous, skilful leaders seize the opportunity to change things for the better"

― Harry S. Truman

Change and Leadership share a symbiotic relationship. Neither can do without the other, and both are indispensable to progress. This book aims to provide the reader with a sound understanding of various concepts related to organisational change, while serving as a practical guide to mitigating resistance to change. It elucidates how effective leadership is essential to steer organisations through strategic changes, and makes the CEO the focal point of initiating and driving change successfully throughout the organisation.

"The Art of Change Management" begins with an introductory chapter on change, which gives a panoramic view of organisational change, the various forms it can take, the change drivers, the role of leadership in change; and also shares with the reader the broad context of organisational change. From there, it takes a structured look into the change process, breaking it into different phases and analyzing the process of change implementation in terms of role clarification, identification of priorities, creation of action plans, execution and evaluation.

Next, it addresses a very vital aspect of change – Resistance. While resistance is common as a response to change, this section dissects resistance to give the reader an understanding of what people are resistant to and why they are resistant. Additionally, it puts together a set of best practices that help to overcome resistance and use it as strength, rather than have it pose as an obstacle to the change process.

It moves on with detailed discussions on the role of top management in engineering change, the use of various change management strategies and the importance of effective communication during change.

Thereafter, the spotlight shifts entirely on the CEO's role in change. Subsequent sections handle questions regarding what the CEO can bring to the table when it comes to change, and how CEO attributes can impact organisational change. Through a set of interesting revelations, this book brings to the reader researched results from various surveys conducted across the globe, with the objective of drawing attention to factors that can be consciously managed to ensure best results. Further, it studies the role of the CEO in Succession Planning – a transition that can literally make or break an organisation – and the responsibility of which rests, at least in part, on the wisdom of the CEO.

And finally, it brings to the reader some of the most able CEOs of industry giants like Xerox, Infosys, P&G etc. who led successful change efforts across their organisations, driving home the point that change, although apparently difficult, is ultimately integral to growth. For, as Gail Sheehy said - If we don't change, we don't grow. If we don't grow, we aren't really living.

Percy Agreras Dastur

CHAPTER 1 /

Introduction to Change

Your success in life isn't based on your ability to simply change.

It is based on your ability to change faster than your competition, customers and business.

~ Mark Sanborn ~

"That's ok, Marcus. But the appraisals! Why should he have to get involved in our appraisals?"

"And come to think of it. We are already neck deep in backlogs. What sense do you see in this daily data and report submission, Marcus? I mean to do all that everyday would mean precious time lost on actual delivery to the client. Correct me if I'm wrong!"

"Listen, Chris, I understand your concerns. And yours too Genevieve and no, you're not wrong anywhere. But understand this now and understand this well. If you want to survive the market, this Change is going to be inevitable. We need the resources and we have no choice but to accept his terms."

Genevieve's mouth opened, and then dropped. And for the first time, Chris looked away, seemingly nonchalant yet, Marcus knew, deeply concerned. "God, I hope I'm not losing the support of my closest associates. Not now," he thought.

....

The maxim "Change is the only constant in life" is easier reiterated than implemented. More often than not, the knowledge that an organisational Change warrants a Change in your own self can set off an uneasy feeling. But to know that an organisation can seldom avoid Change can also help to offset that feeling and help view organisational Changes from a whole new perspective.

ORGANISATIONAL CHANGE: WHAT IS IT?

A Change across the organisation that impacts one or more dimensions of its functioning, such as staffing, structuring, work allocation or turnouts etc. is referred to as an organisational Change. This is opposed to smaller Changes such as isolated personnel movements, modifying a program, using a new computer procedure etc.

When I was a toddler, a red ball in the last shop on the lane was all I ever dreamt of possessing. After some time, I was packed off and sent to school in a nice new uniform. I yelped, I cried, I kicked around, but I soon realized that that would not help. "How will you grow up if you don't go to school?" sermons were fed every day and eventually, I understood that like Fred, Tom, Harry and any other kid down the block, this Change for me was inevitable.

I grew up some more. Now, there was a new thing that occupied my life - the annual tennis tournament. I practiced day in and day out and the only thing I dreamt of was to beat

Glenn in the tournament. By the time I went to college, I had set a new record, broken that and set a new one again. Then life got tougher. I knew that to survive, I needed to find work fast. And then, when I finally found work, I realized after a couple of years that I wanted more opportunities to diversify my skill set. And so I struggled, went to work even with no pay to learn new stuff, to improve, to upgrade.

Today, when I look back, I realize that from the red ball to the tournament to the first job and to all those that followed, I grew, I evolved, I Changed - according to my priorities in life. From one phase of life to another, it was this Change that helped me grow as an individual.

With an organisation too, it is much the same. Every company passes through various phases of evolution, identifying challenges, targeting customers, setting goals, achieving them, raising the bar, and so bit by bit, climbing on to the top. In the process, Change is inevitable.

Of course, this is the most basic Change driver that we are talking about. In the kind of global economy that we ride today, there are a plethora of such drivers, some of which come home through repercussion effects of significant Changes in foreign lands and some that are driven by industry best practices or catering to surviving competition.

That said, once we accept that organisational Changes are practically inevitable, the focus shifts on intelligently handling Change, at an individual as well as at an organisational level, to ensure that it turns out the best results. Indeed, in the attempt to score greater heights, Change management is a much more important link than we often reckon. And to be able to properly manage Change, it pays to know the various types of Changes that can confront an organisation.

TYPES OF ORGANISATIONAL CHANGE

And for the first time, Marcus walked back to his cabin, feeling cut off from his crew, from Chris and Genevieve and Martha and...the team he had so laboriously built up and reared. CEO of a small startup with 10 odd people, Marcus I-Systems was a dream that was fast blowing to bits. Between lost projects, client grievances, resource crunches and low funding, he had just enough time to breathe every day. For months now, Marcus had been frantically hunting for an investor, with little luck and when he had finally found an anchor, happy and relieved at last, his employees back home had been far from excited.

"Mr. Vincent's on the line, Sir. And he'd like to check if we're ready to go live yet?" his CRO's voice buzzed in.

Marcus closed his eyes and thought.

"No we aren't. Tell him we aren't ready, Sue!" he had yelled, mentally. "We aren't ready to go live today. Any day. We're dying!"

Why is Change always so difficult? Experts classify Change into 3 broad groups as Type I, Type II and Type III Change.

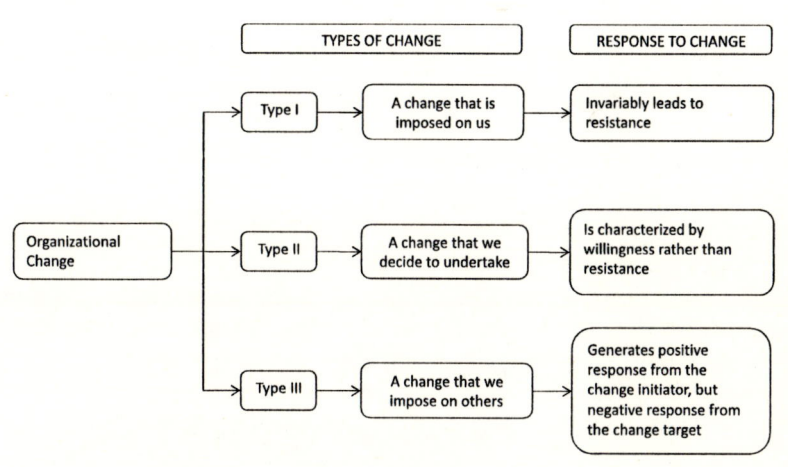

Organizational Change	Types of Change		Response to Change
	Type I	A change that is imposed on us	Invariably leads to resistance
	Type II	A change that we decide to undertake	Is characterized by willingness rather than resistance
	Type III	A change that we impose on others	Generates positive response from the change initiator, but negative response from the change target

Figure 1.1 – Classification of Organisational Change

The Type I Change is a Change that others impose on us. And it is a Change we all resist, because to some extent, it intrudes into our independence.

A Type II Change is one that we impose on ourselves. This may not be easy to implement, all the same, but is definitely a decision that is taken by ourselves and for ourselves. So the resistance is considerably less.

A Type III Change is one that we impose on others.

In any given "Change situation" all three occur simultaneously depending on the viewer's perspective. For instance, Marcus was initiating a Type II Change by choosing to bring in a new investor to his company. But, in the process, he was also imposing on his employees a Change in terms of their future responsibilities and working relationships. A Type III Change from Marcus's perspective, but a Type I Change from the perspective of his employees. When attempting to implement a Type I Change, management needs to communicate the Change as clearly as possible so that employees are correct in their beliefs regarding how much control they have over the process and wherever possible, always give some control of the Change to those who must respond to it.

Where most organisations typically err is that they assume that a Type II Change for them is a Type II for everyone else and that makes Change all the more difficult. Put simply,

I am trying to say that the first condition to engineer a Change smoothly is to put yourself in place of the one you are imposing a Change on. Look from the other person's perspective to see if you can help ease some of his concerns, mitigate some of his fears. Remember, Change is never easy. But the way you handle it could make it a lot less difficult for the one on the receiving end. It is worth noting, that if the statement "People resist Change" were true, then Type II Change would exist only on rare occasions. Nonetheless, if we look around us, most of the big Changes we endure are all self inflicted; marriage; children; learning a new language; acquiring any new skill; etc. etc. All of these are Changes we choose to embrace. Deciding to Change is easy when we realize we must Change, the challenge is to maintain that decision when progress becomes difficult.

Theoretically, organisational Changes have often been classified as:

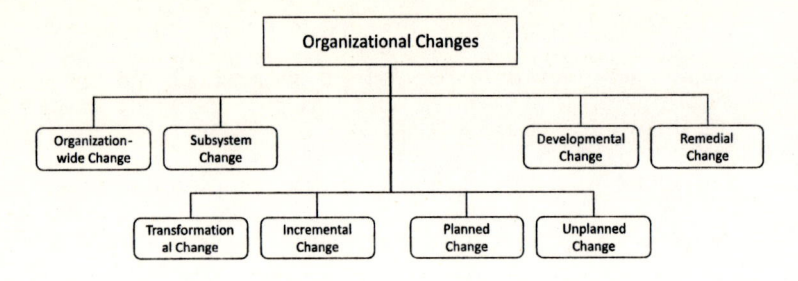

```
                    Organizational Changes
         ┌──────────────┼──────────────┐
    ┌────┴────┐                   ┌────┴────┐
Organization- Subsystem      Developmental  Remedial
wide Change    Change           Change       Change
         ┌────┴────┐              ┌────┴────┐
   Transformation Incremental   Planned   Unplanned
     al Change     Change       Change     Change
```

Figure 1.2 – Types of Organisational Change

The organisation-wide Change is one which spans across the entire organisation. So, you may have a restructuring of the organisation, a major collaboration or a shift in work culture as your company evolves through consecutive phases of development. A subsystem Change could be seen in the restructuring of a small department or the introduction of a new product or service etc.

A transformational Change is one which is at once all assuming, fundamental and radical. For instance, a Change in the company's organisation structure from a hierarchical one to one with several self directing teams or a slashing of impact levels etc. On the other hand, an incremental Change is gradual, such as the implementation of a new software or system to augment efficiency.

A developmental Change is one that occurs when a company

wants to better an existing situation or level of performance. A remedial Change on the other hand is suited to correct a current aberration or a poor performance.

A planned Change is one which is undertaken after a concerted decision is taken by the management to proactively adopt a new strategy or effect a structural / functional Change. An unplanned Change is what happens in order to meet an unforeseen contingency.

These classifications however are not watertight. In fact, functionally, it is more important to understand, identify and cope with the Type I, Type II and Type III Changes in order to ensure better Change Management. Now that you know the different types of Change, try considering different aspects of Change.

THE CHANGE DRIVERS

There are many factors that drive Change across an organisation. Broadly, we may label them as External Change Drivers and Internal Change Drivers. The distinct classification in to External and Internal Change Drivers provides a notion that there are two varying schedules for Change. However, the internal drivers may materialize from external drivers for Change. For example, if clients are becoming more challenging, an External Change Driver, then, internally it would necessitate improvement in the quality of products and services, or an improvement in the innovation process itself.

Organisations are driven to Change due to external, strategic drivers. But at the same time there is always an operational context that has to be taken into account. To manage Change successfully, there is a need for a focus on both strategic and operational issues, with both being closely linked.

The External Change Drivers could surface in the form of a global trend. For instance, the global recession that hit the markets in the year 2009. Experts claimed that in terms of global business, the 2009 disaster was as bad as the cataclysm of World War II or the 1930's Great Depression. It led to massive job cuts and unemployment, with practically every sector being affected, from autos and airlines to pharmaceuticals and consumer products, not to forget technology. In the global economy that we operate in, repercussion effects of a currency crisis in another country is another significant source of Change. Factors like how other organisations in a particular industry function, a shift in industry best practices, or a shift in the demand with changing fashions etc. could also impact the functioning of an organisation and trigger a Change

An important observation from the global recession of 2009, however, has been that different companies have felt the heat differently. While some companies like Microsoft and Caterpillar drastically cut jobs during this period, there were others who were better equipped to handle Change and survive pressures because of a strong brand loyalty or a flexible cost structure etc.

In fact, many times it is seen that external drivers of Change expose internal inefficiencies that lead to Change. Caterpillar, the world's largest manufacturer of construction and mining machines, for instance, had announced 20,000 job cuts because it was unable to sustain the high operating costs, when the market collapse slashed its sales volume by some 25%. This brings us to internal agents of Change.

Internal Change Drivers may include a Change in funding, resource constraints or new mergers, introduction of new product or service, a new CEO, and an array of other factors. Most internal Change also happens as a result of a shift in the organisation's evolution from a reactive to a proactive stage. These Changes are introduced with a view to steer developments. Of course, organisation wide Change can also be corrective or preventive rather than developmental in nature, as when the need for immediate mitigation of a current crisis steers the Change.

BROAD CONTEXT FOR ORGANISATIONAL CHANGE AND DEVELOPMENT

What Drives Change?

The stimulants for organisational Change could be many. Organisational Changes occur, for instance, when an organisation Changes its overall strategy for success, adds or removes a major section or practice, or Changes its operating techniques. Usually organisational Change is provoked by external forces, for instance to address the need for an increase in productivity or services in response to new clients. Organisational Changes may stem from a Change in mission, a restructuring of operations, introduction of a new product or service, layoffs sparked by internal or external contingencies, new technologies, merger and acquisitions, new programs such as Total Quality Management and the list goes on. But generally, whatever the reason, a move to Change is always tailored to either correct a situation or to move to a higher level of functioning.

Every Change therefore is a strategy to accomplish a concrete vision, a meta goal. Ideally, an organisation must plan out an organisation-wide Change in order to evolve to the next life cycle level and thus ensuring to move from an organisation which is highly reactive to a more stable and proactive organisation, an organisation which is also entrepreneurial in its approach ensuring planned development.

Why is it Difficult to Accomplish Change in an Organisation?

Whoever said "Change is the elixir of life" could not have met with a bigger antithesis. Change is almost always perceived as a negative threat.

It is common human psychology to prefer an existing set of unfavorable conditions than to graduate to a potential set of favorable but unknown conditions. So, typically for every proposed Change, there is always an equal and opposite resistance acting against it.

Another very basic reason why Change is difficult to

accomplish in an organisation or why people resist Change is related to the way our mind works. Typically, when a person engages himself in any activity, a larger part of his work is handled by the subconscious mind, and only a minuscule part of it is attended to by his active mind. The active mind satisfies itself by ideating on what is new, in any given task, while the subconscious mind performs the larger routine roles embedded in that task. Now, the subconscious mind is pre programmed in the performance of these routine tasks, by virtue of repetition and habit. When a Change is proposed, the subconscious mind faces an implicit threat, because the Change poses a reprogramming, a new way of doing things that have habitually been done in a different manner. For e.g. the implementation of SAP HR in a company's human resource activities, which were earlier done manually. Now, this Change is definitely a positive one, yet it does not bring in the desired results. Why? Because the business human resource managers are resistant to this Change. They would rather continue with the old way of doing things manually because they are habituated with it. In other words, they resist this Change because it requires them to unlearn and relearn, because it requires them to Change the way they are accustomed to do things. So, many times it is not that they resist the actual Change. Rather, they resist the implied

Change that the actual Change is empowered to trigger off in them, by changing their habits, values or mode of functioning and thinking.

Specifically, an organisation wide Change, is often difficult to accomplish because not only are people cynical of Change, they are also afraid of it. Many doubt the effectiveness of strategies aiming at major Changes. Often, organisation wide Changes are stalled because of conflicting goals within the organisation. A certain move, for instance, could require more investment in terms of resources whereas the company may be on an austerity drive, fanatically cutting costs. Another important factor is the cultural shift that such a Change warrants, in terms of what the employees value and consider as correct or best.

Role of Top Management in Steering Change

For successful implementation, Change needs to be driven by the top level management. It is important that an individual or a group to consciously perceive, ideate, spearhead and accomplish the Change.

Change is usually best carried out as a team effort. Not only does this imply that each and every individual in the team is intimately associated with the Change, it also means that there is a proper connect between individual and group goals. Also, communicating the Change and the concomitant goals appropriately to employees across the organisation is crucial.

A Change is best managed when you can genuinely win your employees to your reason for effecting the Change. If the Change has been conceived to impact the organisation and its people favorably, then communicating the same in an appropriate manner helps to build mutual trust and confidence. Once people are clear on why a Change is required, they will want to know the how to steer the Change. At this stage, it is important to allow open exchange of ideas and concerns, rather than issuing diktats. Not only will this help to gain a more holistic appreciation of the desired Change, it will also help empower people at lower levels to take decisions or come up with suggestions.

Guidelines to Successfully Accomplish Change

There are many approaches to maneuver Change, but broadly speaking, you may choose to work either forward towards a vision or backwards to address a current situation. While the former involves visioning and then planning and streamlining your actions to attain that vision, the latter involves identifying current priorities, focus area or pain areas, and then action planning about to how to address them.

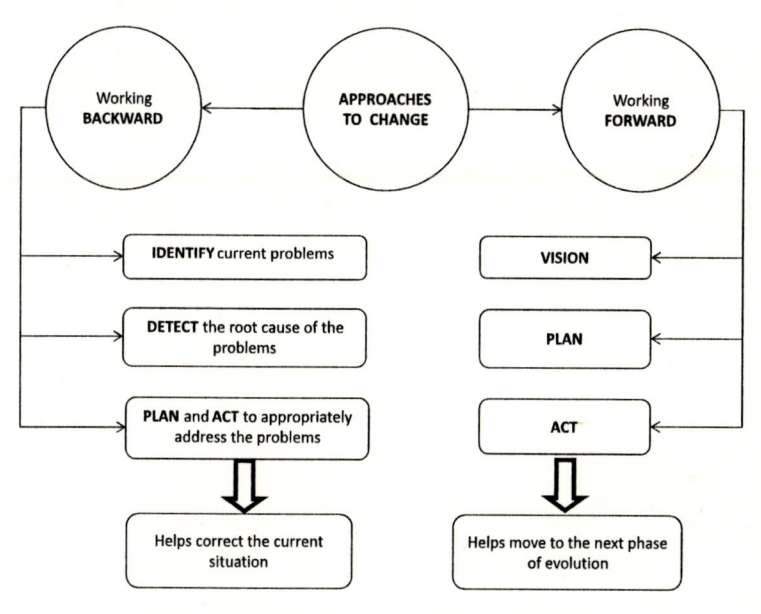

```
                    Working BACKWARD  ←  APPROACHES TO CHANGE  →  Working FORWARD

                    IDENTIFY current problems                    VISION
                    DETECT the root cause of the problems        PLAN
                    PLAN and ACT to appropriately address        ACT
                    the problems
                    ⇩                                            ⇩
                    Helps correct the current situation          Helps move to the next phase of evolution
```

Figure 1.3 – Approaches to Change

The watchword therefore is proper planning on how you want to reach your goals, how long might it take and how will you measure your progress? In the meanwhile, even as you effect a Change in your organisation take care that it does not adversely impact the functioning of your customers or clients.

Include the group impacted by the change party to it by including them in the policy making. While you make out a policy to carry out a preplanned Change, try to identify groups that will be most affected by the Change. Include them or their representatives while policy making to steer this Change. This way, when the Change is actually driven across the organisation, they themselves feel party to the Change. This eases out the resistance to Change and helps in bringing about a smooth transition.

You could also plan to hire the services of an experienced consultant to help you successfully guide and implement Change.

CHANGE AND THE ROLE OF A LEADER

As a leader or a manager, your role in initiating, driving and sustaining Change is of paramount importance. As a leader, you definitely have a wider spectrum of experience and knowledge to draw upon. Additionally, try to look around and discover ideas, that have worked with other people and that might fit your situation. Stretch your horizons, conceive possibilities, ideate. In business, we cannot stagnate. And to keep moving, you need to show visible improvement.

Improvement comes from the implementation of a positive Change, however that Change needs to be first envisioned

You, as a leader are equipped best not only to conceive the Change, but also to drive the Change. Generally, everyone has some latent or dormant potential that is yet unexplored. Identify and coach this talent, build a team that believes in and can drive the Change. Additionally, your responsibility does not end with coaching and setting people to work. Rather, help your people see possibilities. Empower them to make decisions, encourage them to come up with their own perspectives. Your real ability as a leader lies in discovering and molding the leader in the person who least expects to.

CHAPTER 2 /

The Change Process

Keep in mind that you cannot control your own future. Your destiny is not in your hands; it is in the hands of the irrational consumer and society. The changes in their needs, desires, and demands will tell you where you must go. All this means that managers must themselves feel the pulse of change on a daily, continuous basis.... They should have intense curiosity, observe events, analyze trends, seek the clues of change, and translate those clues into opportunities.

~ Michael J. Kami ~

"I'm quitting!" Marcus heard an exasperated Chris in his cabin.

Visibly, far from being excited at the possibility of a potential handsome investment, Chris had not quite liked the idea of another boss and a ton more of workload! And so hadn't anyone, it seemed...

Marcus looked out of the window. The company had done hopelessly poor business in the last few months, and he had taken it upon himself to ensure that he could bring in the required resources to end this crunch. And he had done it. Done it all alone!

But what good was it if he had to pay a price by losing the support of his people? Hadn't he built his company on the ideal that his people relationships would always remain his greatest strength? Then how could he hope to survive when his biggest strength was crumbling? Or had he gone wrong somewhere?

He closed his eyes. His moment of ultimate achievement, relief, and happiness was turning into a disaster!

To avoid a disaster, it pays to know the Change Process and manage Change accordingly. Where Marcus went wrong was that he accomplished the entire organisation wide Change, without considering the impact of the Change in role and expectations or discussing the same with those who would be directly affected by it.

Typically, the Change Process can be divided into four phases for effective implementation. However, these phases are not watertight compartments, so you may combine or split some phases, to respond to your specific purposes.

PHASES OF THE CHANGE PROCESS

- PHASE I - Clarifying Roles and Expectations of Employees during and after the Change Process

- PHASE II - Identify Change Priorities

- PHASE III – Plan Organisational Development Activities (ODA's) according to identified priorities

- PHASE IV - Effectively Manage and Evaluate Change

The Art of Change Management

Phase I — Clarify roles and expectations during the change process
- Identify your official, direct and indirect Clients
- Define Indicators for measuring Project Success
- Clarify changes in roles/ expectations accordingly

Phase II — Identify change priorities
- Build a project team to study the existing situation
- Collect relevant Data
- Analyze the data to identify change priorities and come up with recommendations to initiate change

Phase III — Plan ODA's according to identified priorities
- Translate recommendations into ODA's
- Devise an action plan to accomplish the ODA's
- Plan your ODA's according to the priorities identified in Phase II

Phase IV — Effectively Manage and evaluate change
- Communicate the Action Plan to all concerned
- Implement Action Plan
- Undertake training programmes and revaluate your success indicators periodically
- Confirm project success by tallying project outcomes against pre defined indicators and project goals

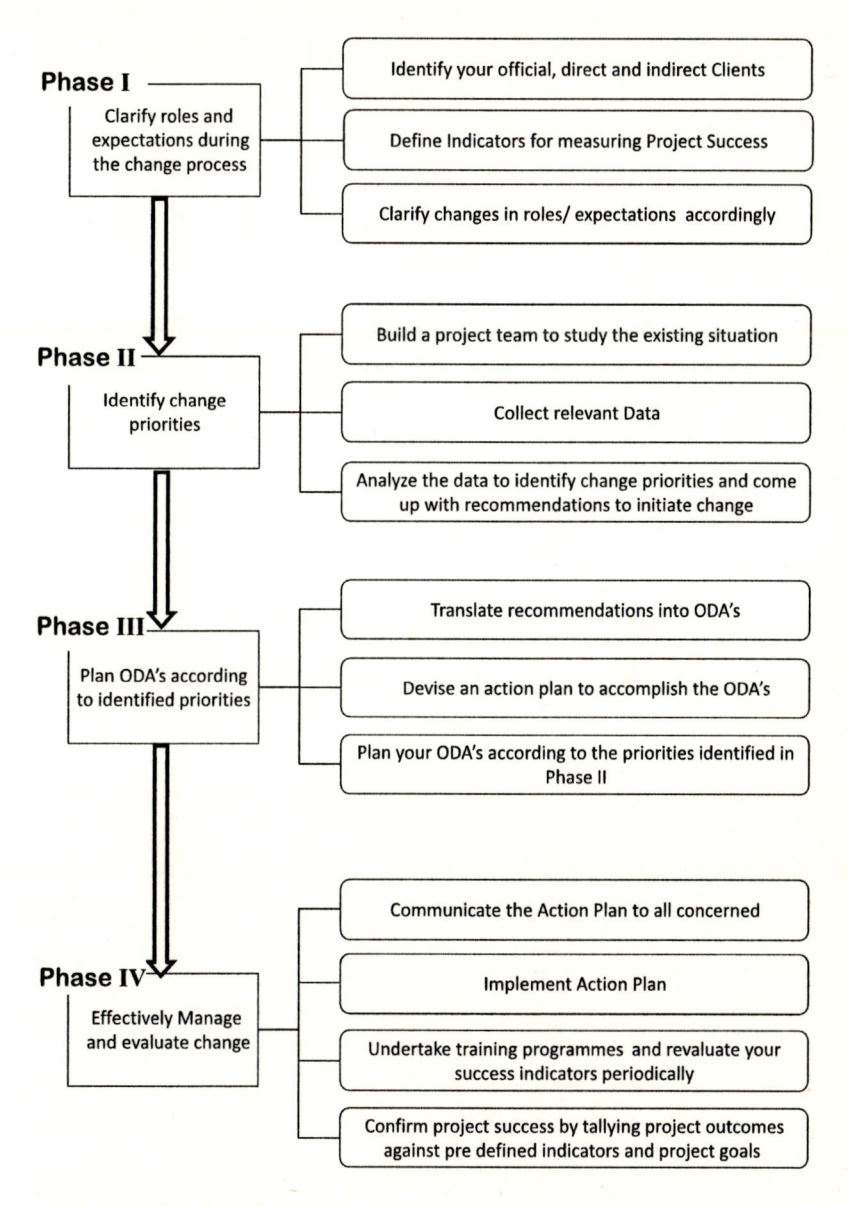

Figure 2.1-The Change Process

PHASE I: ADDRESSING CLARIFICATIONS RELATED TO ROLES AND EXPECTATIONS FOR CHANGE PROCESS

Whenever we talk of Change in the context of an organisation, the first thing to understand is that it implies a Change in the roles and expectations of the people involved. To provide a clear picture of this role Change, you need to have an understanding of the following:

I. Client Identification

As the Change agent or the one driving the Change, your first task therefore is to identify your clients. Experts classify three different categories of clients you might need to deal with.

```
CLIENT CATEGORIES

Your Client ──► Official    ──► He assigns to you the responsibility of driving the change
           ──► Direct       ──► He works with you to implement the change
           ──► Indirect Client ──► He is indirectly influenced by the change you make
```

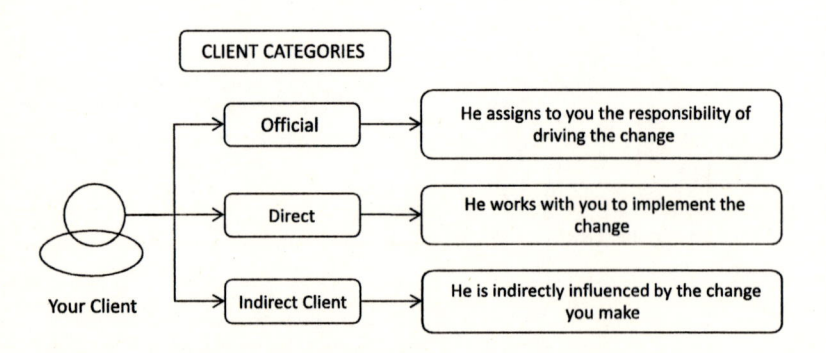

Figure 2.2 – Different Types of Client Categories

Official Client: The official client is the one who assigns to you the responsibility of driving the Change. Identify your official client and ensure that at every stage in the Change process, you keep him updated on the progress of your assignment. Take his feedback from time to time on the way things are headed.

Direct Client: Your direct clients involve all those with whom you collaborate to bring about the Change assigned to you by your official client. For instance, your manager may have assigned you the Change project, so he is your direct client. But to achieve that Change, you need to collaborate with your immediate colleagues and one or more third parties. So they become your direct clients. Direct Clients are the people with whom you interact closely and regularly, so they are the strongest links that can help you bring about Change. It is important to clarify to your direct clients, in concrete terms, the Change that you are looking at, the reason for wanting this Change, the time frame within which to accomplish the Change, the indicators to measure success and their role in bringing about this Change. Strive to ensure that you genuinely include each and every direct client in the process by considering their feedback, allowing them to voice their concerns and encouraging them to become owners of specific areas of the Change implementation. Work towards a relationship of mutual trust and respect and make them party to the Change rather than making them feel that they are merely carrying out orders. This helps to create a level of satisfaction among them for being able to engineer the Change rather than being used as tools to bring about a Change.

Indirect Client: Your Indirect Clients are those who are indirectly but ultimately influenced by the Changes you make. They could be internal or external to the organisation. But it is important that they agree in principle with the end result of your Change project.

II. Identification of Indicators that define Project Success

1. Try to identify quantitative indicators to measure the success of the project. Even if the end result is a qualitative Change, establishing quantitative indicators help in understanding the progress and ultimately the success of the project. Arrive at a common understanding with your official client as to what these indicators are. Once this is done, you have better role clarity for your direct clients.

2. Try re-evaluating your project goals from time to time.

Often, while steering Change towards a defined result, you and your client may realize that to attain that end result, you need to address a more important or basic problem. In such a situation, you must Change your project parameters accordingly for a more holistic and sustainable result to set in.

3. Try completing the project within the defined budget and time.

4. If you are an external consultant who has been hired by an official client, you can judge the success of your project at a personal level by taking count of the relationship that you have build with your client during the course of the project or whether both of you would like a long term relationship etc.

PHASE II: IDENTIFYING PRIORITIES OF CHANGE

Once you have identified your clients and defined the indicators, you are ready to start your work. As a first step, to visualize the extent of Change required, you need to know the gap between the existing situation and the desired situation because your project is meant precisely to bridge this gap. Follow the simple steps given below to conduct an appropriate research on the current situation that helps you zero in on your priorities:

1. **Establish a Project Team:** Form a small team, comprising about six to eight people, who are sincere, knowledgeable in their functional areas and also possess a basic understanding of the organisational context for the Change, and set them to collect data that help visualize the current situation. The CEO and Board Chair could be important, often necessary players on your team. With their knowledge of the history of the organisation, their foresight and their decision making ability, they can help guide your research to yield the most relevant results. Having them onboard is also an advantage because most of the time, it is their vision you are trying to give shape to, so having them as part of your research team means you never lose sight of the ultimate goal, while you are conducting preliminary research. Also, include representative direct clients in your research team.

2. **Data Collection:** Plan and conduct your data collection, according to your project parameters. Use different modes such as documentation reviews, interviews, questionnaires,

surveys, observation, focus groups or case studies to derive best results.

3. **Interpretation of results:** Jointly analyze your findings to identify priorities. Also, try and look for causal connections between different parameters. This will help to provide an optimum starting point to your project. Thus, you and your official client need to work together during this phase to understand priorities of the Change effort and decide how you all can effectively address it.

Once you have identified your project priorities, you must ensure that the results permeate across all your direct clients, so the efforts of the entire team is streamlined towards a single defined objective, at various stages in the project.

PHASE III: PLANNING THE ORGANISATIONAL DEVELOPMENT ACTIVITIES TO ADDRESS THE IDENTIFIED PRIORITIES

Once you are through with research and identification of priorities, you will realize that in the process you have probably come up with recommendations of various activities that can be taken up across departments and levels to bring about the desired Change. Next, you need to decide an action plan to implement the recommendations. So, basically to start off with, there are three things to do after identification of priorities:

A. To translate the recommendations arrived upon during your research into defined activities. These activities are termed as Organisation Development Activities or Interventions or Capacity Building Activities.

B. To devise an action plan to accomplish these activities.

C. To plan these activities according to your priorities, as revealed during the research.

A. Translating Recommendations into ODA's

When you decide upon your Organisation Development Activities, it pays to keep the following factors in mind:

1. The time frame you have at your disposal, within which the Change has to be accomplished.

2. The resources and talent that you have at your disposal.

3. The organisation culture and whether your activities are consistent with that culture.

4. The Change management strategy, if one is used. For instance, if you are using a strategic management plan, then you may have to undertake a SWOT analysis to decide upon your strategic goals, which will in turn influence your developmental activities to be undertaken.

5. Also, you need to know the "lens" through which you view your organisation. If you view your organisation from a structural perspective, then you might select ODA's that correspond to roles, responsibilities, policies, procedures, hierarchy, control etc. If you view it from an HR perspective, your activities will tend to respond to communication, relationships, fulfillment, participation, needs of people, enrichment etc.

SOME ODA'S OR INTERVENTIONS THAT ORGANISATIONS CHOOSE:

While organisations choose their ODA's broadly according to the Change they wish to drive, some of the common interventions that can be integrated into the Change process to bring about an all round development are listed below:

Human Process Interventions

With growing emphasis on human relations, human process interventions are increasingly being integrated with other capacity building activities to ensure a holistic Change process, wherein the people in the organisation can enhance themselves and enrich the way they work.

This kind of an intervention is especially useful when a company has many new employees, or a mix of cultures working together, conflicts, low morale, or ineffective teams, etc. These interventions include:

Guiding Individuals – This initiative involves coaching, counseling, mentoring and motivating individuals. It also involves appropriate delegation of work and stress management.

Group-Based Guidance – This initiative involves Group learning, creation of self directed teams, dialoguing, conflict management etc.

Techno - Structural Interventions

Interventions that are directed towards improving the performance of organisations by modifying structures, technologies, operations, procedures and roles/positions in the organisation are called Techno-Structural Interventions.

These include approaches such as Six Sigma, Total Quality Management, and Business Process Re-Engineering etc. Techno - Structural interventions might be particularly helpful when your internal systems are not sufficient to sustain the rapid growth in your organisation or when you confront many complaints from customers, etc.

Human Resource Management Interventions

Developmental activities that are undertaken to enhance overall organisational performance by improving the performance of individuals and teams within the organisation are called Human Resource Management Interventions.

They include the following Initiatives:

> **Employee Per**formance Management – This consists of defining performance goals, performance contracts and plans, performance evaluation, performance rewarding, development plans etc.

Employee Development – This involves developing a career path for employees of the organisation, undertaking personal development, leadership development, management development programs or training and development programs etc.

Human Resource Interventions can be beneficially integrated into your Change project when new organisational goals have been established, a major new system requires timely implementation or you are grappling with ineffective teams or lack of role clarity, appropriate job description etc.

Strategic Interventions

Those activities that are undertaken in response to external business environment, for instance a global recession, increase in competition, market expansion, mergers and acquisitions etc. are known as strategic interventions.

Strategic interventions can be profitably integrated into your Change project to address situations where there have been rapid Changes in the external environment, or sales figures have surged or plunged abnormally in response to external factors etc.

B. Devising an Action Plan

Next comes devising an action plan. Your action plan is built around specific activities, but it could have a more or less similar format. Take care to include the following while devising an action plan for best results:

1. Clearly define the goal.

2. Lay down the precise strategy that you are adopting to reach that goal.

3. If need be, mention specific objectives to be addressed as sub parts of the overall strategy.

4. Most importantly, assign specific responsibilities or objectives to each direct client or group of direct clients.

5. Also define the timeline within which the objective has to be accomplished.

Undertake a suitable program evaluation from time to time to ensure that your concerted efforts are headed in the right direction.

C. To plan these activities according to your priorities, as revealed during the research

Once you have completed devising your action plan, ensure that you execute the actions according to the priorities concluded in Phase II.

PHASE IV: CHANGE MANAGEMENT & EVALUATION

The last phase of the Change Process involves sustaining and evaluating the action plans, including management of resistance to Change, which may come from various sources, sometimes from the Change agent as well, as in the case of a project termination! The following are some simple steps to see you through the last bit of your Change process:

Communication of Action plan - Once you have figured out your action plan, the next step is to communicate the plan, so all those involved in steering the Change stand on a level ground.

Implementation of Action Plans – In order to ensure that your plans are implemented, you as the leader or change agent need to provide the major initial push. To facilitate the action plan, start off with getting your team mates to know each other. After all, they are expected to deliver the best results as a team and building a team rapport is as important as getting the team to work. Further down the line, you need to clearly discuss your aims, budgets, timelines and other important guidelines governing the project. There are various methods you could apply to get the ball rolling. Start with a face-to-face meeting to introduce your members and make an impact yourself. Subsequently, depending upon the time at disposal, you may plan virtual meetings, teleconferences or communicate through emails. But, whatever the mode, take care to ensure that you keep the communication going. Not only will this help you to keep a regular tab on the progress and implementation of your project, it will also help interaction among your team members and facilitate a stronger group effort directed towards a common objective.

Undertake Training, Coaching and Motivational sessions to spruce up your progress - You, as a leader can influence the quality of work that your team delivers. Take time out to motivate, train and coach your players. Delegate work, and most importantly manage stress intelligently. Also, devise a training strategy for your team mates and supervisors. Training is crucial for building knowledge about the Change and the required skills. Project team members need to develop training requirements based on the skill sets and knowledge necessary to implement the Change. These training requirements will be then be used to develop streamlined training programs.

Evaluation of Project Activities and Desired Results – Finally evaluate your progress periodically against established indicators, and share the results with your members, to maximize your chances of success.

CHAPTER 3 /

Resistance To Change

Change can either challenge or threaten us... Your beliefs pave your way to success or block you.

~ Marsha Sinetar ~

Marcus quickly collected himself. "No..." he thought."I cannot let this happen!"

Venturing out of his cabin, Marcus felt for the first time, voices being hushed up and sideways glances stealing abhorrent looks at him. No one had come up to his cabin since the announcement and there was no explicit showdown, as he had feared. But the air reeked of turbulence. It pained him!

Over the next few hours, he tried connecting with his most trusted associates, in an attempt to gauge the reaction. He was met with diverse responses. Cathy and Joe were unusually quiet, meek perhaps. Chris, as usual, was ranting but was open in his communication. Marcus could not help but think that a few issues that concerned Chris had indeed slipped his mind. "Would it have been better if I had spoken to him earlier? Perhaps...."

Later that day, Chris found a new mail in his inbox, just as he was preparing to leave office. He was generally the last one to go. "Meeting at 12.00 p.m. in the conference room tomorrow. We need to talk about the proposed Change I mentioned earlier in the day. Your opinion is important and I will take a final call only after we discuss this in greater detail...You make a difference and always will." - Marcus had written.

Though the events of the day had left him in awe and disgust, the last line resonated with Chris. He knew Marcus meant it.

As for Marcus, Chris did mean a lot to him. And so did Martha, Steve and Genevieve.... and Sue and Cathy and Joe and.....How could he work without their support? Once he was done sending that email to one and all, he clicked 'shutdown'... Tomorrow would be a new day, he thought.

....

RESISTANCE TO ORGANISATIONAL CHANGE INITIATIVES

Indeed, Change is seldom a welcome proposition. U.S. radical activist, Saul Alinsky, hit the nail on the head, when he said -

"Change means movement. Movement means friction. Only in the frictionless vacuum of a nonexistent abstract world can movement or Change occur without that abrasive friction of conflict."

This is particularly true in context of an organisation. In Chapter 1, we discussed the various stimulants, internal and external, which can trigger organisational Changes, and saw that almost always, they are necessary for the development of the organisation. Yet, more often than not, organisational

Change initiatives are met with apprehension and resistance.

Hence, a large part of effective Change management depends on how well people reactions to Change are managed. As the driving force of the organisation, the CEO plays a significant role here - not only in visualizing a Change, but also in preparing his people to embrace that Change. His initiatives can go a long way to ensure that the Change Process not only helps the organisation to evolve but also enables its people to enrich and expand their frontiers of thinking.

There are two ways of going about a Change process. You visualize and decide upon a Change, you delegate the work it calls upon to your subordinates, they follow your dictates and the Change is accomplished. OR you visualize a Change, you carry people along in your vision and make them part of the thought process, you open their eyes to a whole new world of possibilities and then encourage them to ideate ways of engineering the Change. In the second option, not only have you minimized the possibilities of resistance, but at the end of the day, you also have a people strength that is more involved, more satisfied and more capable of steering such Change in future. The trick lies not in filling an empty bucket with water but in genuinely lighting a spark. And that is where the CEO can make a difference.

REACTIONS TO CHANGE

"Change has a considerable psychological impact on the human mind. To the fearful it is threatening because it means that things may get worse. To the hopeful it is encouraging because things may get better. To the confident it is inspiring because the challenge exists to make things better."

— *King Whitney, Jr.*

Any Change initiative can give rise to a gamut of reactions from resistance to disinterestedness to willingness to accept the Change. Creation of a potentially better work environment, the thrill of being able to participate in something different and an expansion of the current set of opportunities can all aid in creating a positive response towards Change. But the most common response to Change, which is also the most harmful response, is that of resistance.

One of the causes of resistance lies in a very basic psychological fact. An external Change demands an internal Change, and while most of us can understand that in a world of uncertainty

Change is irrepressible, most of us hate to Change our own selves to be able to respond to the Change in circumstances.

Human beings have an immense capacity for perception and sensitivity. Think about it, you can smell a few drops of perfume across the entire house, you can feel that mosquito on you when it's still some distance away, and you can gauge emotions without words. Then why do we block our sensitivity and perception when it comes to accepting Change. Why can't we see beyond boundaries and discern possibilities that most often, are meant to unlock the best in us? Why do we resist Change intrinsically?

```
                    ┌─────────────────────────┐
                    │  RESISTANCE TO CHANGE   │
                    └─────────────────────────┘
                         │            │
          ┌──────────────┘            └──────────────┐
          ▼                                          ▼
┌─────────────────────┐                   ┌─────────────────────┐
│     WHAT DO         │                   │   WHY DO EMPLOYEES  │
│ EMPLOYEES RESIST?   │                   │       RESIST?       │
└─────────────────────┘                   └─────────────────────┘
```

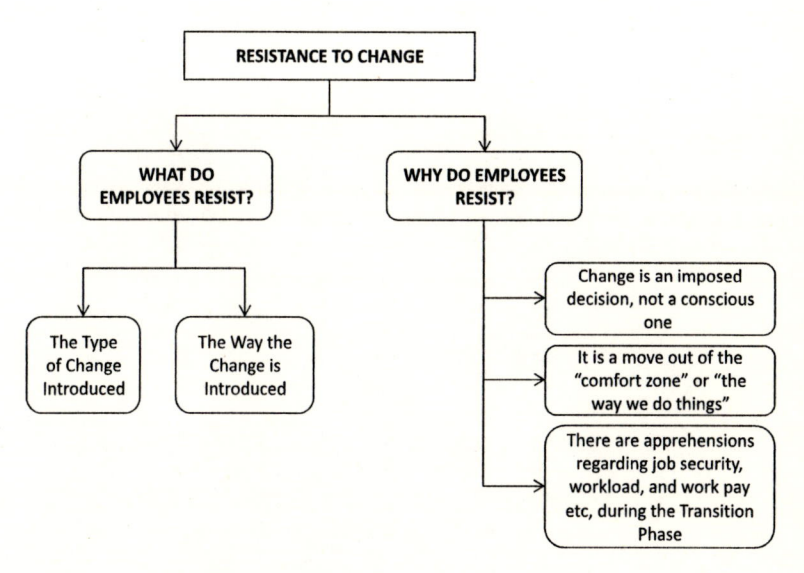

- The Type of Change Introduced
- The Way the Change is Introduced

- Change is an imposed decision, not a conscious one
- It is a move out of the "comfort zone" or "the way we do things"
- There are apprehensions regarding job security, workload, and work pay etc, during the Transition Phase

Figure 3.1 – Resistance to Change

The reason could be that while Change is inevitable, it is not always a conscious decision. Hence, while some may choose to be active participants in the Change process, many may not. This concept is beautifully explained by Scott J. Simmerman's "Teaching the Caterpillar to Fly". Widely regarded as a useful management tool, Dr. Simmerman's initiative explains that while all caterpillars eventually turn into butterflies, much more radiant and beautiful than in their evolutionary phases, most are unaware of the coming Change and he imagines, could be resistant too. Similarly, most people have a lot of latent potential that can propel them to take charge of a higher situation. But many may not be aware of the potential they possess. Hence, they are apprehensive of a Change, which paradoxically may just bring out the best in them!

To understand another aspect of resistance to Change, consider these lines by Ted Forbes, The Darden School of Business:

*"In the Change from being a caterpillar
to becoming a butterfly,
you're nothing more than a yellow,
gooey sticky mess."*

The words are suffused with deep meaning and they open the door to another probable reason why we resist Change – because we hate the discomfort of the transition process.

In the foreseeable future, Change can also come as an end to a familiar way of operating. This gives rise to feelings of insecurity, apprehension, lack of trust in the management etc. These, in turn, induce the employees to resist Change and reinforce the current situation. Visible Changes such as absenteeism or stretching oneself abnormally may occur. While the former occurs as a reaction to seeing older colleagues quit in the face of a Change, the latter results from an urgency to prove oneself in the given situation. Both ways, it shows how individuals become vulnerable in an atmosphere of Change. People may draw away from each other and become self defensive and protective, all this stemming from a feeling of insecurity, and directed towards retaining their own jobs. A sudden Change situation may also see a loss of important workers and hence may result in critical vacancies that need to be filled up as soon as possible, to ensure smooth running of business. Already existing grudges regarding unfair pay, overload of work or bad working relationships can lead to a stressful Change environment, compounding negative attitudes of resistance to Change.

When a Change is announced, employees are generally seen to go through a phase of non acceptance or shock. They may become concerned about their jobs, expectations, hours of work, pay etc. Gradually, as the Change sets in, there is a feeling of anger, resentment or sadness – an environment that is often heavily detrimental productivity and efficiency. However, once the Change becomes part of the system over a period of time, most people learn to accept and adapt themselves to the Changed circumstances, but for those who still can't, a one–to–one interaction with the manager or a mentoring session may help.

Some research results in the area indicate that resistance to organisational Change initiatives can manifest itself in several forms from passivity or indifference to non cooperation in revealing information crucial to data collection phase of the Change process to strikes or violence. In order to effectively handle such reactions, it is also important to understand whether the mass of people is resistant to the type of Change being introduced or whether they are reacting against the way in which the Change is being introduced. Understanding this enables the Change agent to deal with the resistance accordingly.

What influences an employee's attitude to Change?

Research results in the area have projected union membership and organisational commitment as two most important factors that influence attitudes within a Change context. For instance, employees with a high degree of organisational commitment tend to be more supportive to Change, however only to the extent that they don't perceive the Change to be detrimental to their job security.

REASONS FOR AN ORGANISATIONAL FAILURE TO OVERCOME RESISTANCE TO CHANGE

Organisational Change Management has assumed more relevance in recent times, because while Change initiatives are being increasingly introduced across industries, not many of them end up successfully. In the event that a Change initiative fails, the company runs a risk of losing its key employees or senior management and hence it's competitive edge in the market.

This throws up an important question – "What are the reasons for the failure of organisational Change initiatives?" Because of the resistance, you might say. That brings us to another basic question - "What are the reasons for an organisational failure to overcome resistance to Change?" Some common workplace attitudes may help to illuminate the causes why a Change in an organisation is often easier conceived than successfully accomplished:

1. It is a general observation that faced with a problem; we generally try conventional solutions to resolve the same. This is, possibly, to avoid delays due to experimentation, given the restricted time frame available to resolve the problem. This inculcates an attitude of "I know the solution" rather than one of "I discovered a solution." By thinking that we "know" the solution, we often restrict possibilities of other solutions and remain confined within the established boundaries of conventional thought patterns. Naturally, a Change proposed in such an environment conflicts with the convention yet followed, and hence poses a resistance, difficult to overcome.

2. Often, employees are found to be driven by an instinct to "survive" rather than an instinct to "grow". This kind of a complacent attitude makes it difficult to introduce improvement initiatives.

3. Accomplishment of Change initiatives may also become difficult if employees display a lack of trust in the senior

management. It is only when employees enjoy a healthy relationship with the management and is satisfied with the place they work that they tend to support Change initiatives. However, in a survey of 9100 people, Wayson Wyatt concluded that a little more than half of employees are satisfied with their own company and perceive other places as offering better opportunities.

4. The Wyatt Company Work USA Survey (1991) concluded that 88% of executives considered employee participation as important to productivity, yet only 30% felt that their companies were adequately encouraging employee participation in decisions that closely impact them. Even where opinions and suggestions of employees are sought, it was observed that they are seldom acted upon. Not involving the employees as part of your Change vision or initiative can only compound problems of resistance to Change. Common visions and objectives are crucial in defining the success of your Change project. In this direction, the CIPD Research Report indicates that encouraging two-way communication with employees and securing their participation in implementation ensures that they are as much a part of bringing about the Change as they are a part of the impact of the Change.

5. Organisational politics may also hinder Change initiatives in some cases.

6. Often, you may want to import a Change initiative that has worked wonders elsewhere, into your own organisation. However, in such cases it is important to consider factors such as company culture, vision, objectives etc. and then craft a successful Change initiative, which, while being modelled on the initiatives in other companies, appropriately fits your own organisational needs and culture.

To explain such common workplace attitudes that hinder Change initiatives, Dr. Scott J. Simmerman came up with the most interesting "Square Wheels metaphor". To understand this metaphor, imagine to yourself a cart, with square wheels (instead of round ones!), being pushed by two people from behind and pulled by one in the front, to keep it moving forward. As per Simmerman, this cart is also loaded with round wheels.

Figure 3.2: Square Wheels by Dr. Simmerman

This visual has been interpreted in more ways than one to adequately represent an organisational Change situation.

Firstly, the fact that the cart is moving on square wheels illustrates the hard work that it demands from the workers. Yet the fact that the cart is loaded with round wheels points towards the futility of not replacing the square wheels with the round ones for better output. Mapping a correspondence between this situation and an organisational Change situation, Dr. Simmerman opines that most of the time, we operate using inefficient methods that are time consuming, laborious and cost ineffective, when a potential better solution or method can be easily explored. We continue using the inefficient techniques because that is all we know and further because that is all we want to know. Taking a step out of the daily rut challenges are notions of conventional work processes and hence we consciously tend to avoid Change, compounding our troubles in the process.

Going deeper, he analyses that a shift from the "Square Wheels" situation is often not given a thought because even with the square wheels, the cart does manage to progress! Hence, we tend to prefer carrying on with the current process of going about our work, not realising that there might be easier and more effective ways of getting that work done! Another interesting observation he makes is that a cart on square wheels can do your job, but it is difficult for it to Change direction. Thus, he is intelligently brings out the fact that turning towards a prospective better situation becomes difficult when you operate with a "Square Wheels" mindset!

BEST PRACTICES TO OVERCOME RESISTANCE TO CHANGE

I remember once when I was in school - in the seventh grade, I think – how dejected I had felt, when I ended up not being selected as the Class Representative. Not only did this mark an end to a long tradition, what disappointed me more was that the new teacher had preferred Nigel over me…..Nigel!! The most notorious boy across all sections of the seventh standard! It took me a long time to come to an understanding of that choice. Perhaps it was the honor of being made the Class Representative, or the responsibility it brought, but without doubt, in a year's time, Nigel was a Changed personality.

1. Waddell and Sohal in 1998, and later Piderit in 2000 identified resistance as a force or an energy that could actually be redirected to offset barriers to Change, rather than have it serve as a perpetual hindrance to Change. While reactions to Change vary from the passive to the active, the source of resistance is sometimes very conspicuous. For instance an individual or a group may be distinctly overt or vocal about a certain aspect of the Change process. Understand if they are genuinely concerned about a real drawback in the Change process. If so, encourage them to come up with solutions to the problem they have identified. Often planners fail to anticipate issues that people in the function affected can foresee. Once such an issue is identified, people who are most skeptical are often also the best ones to help correct the same. For, after all, a problem seldom comes without a solution!

2. A related point was made by Axelrod, 2002. According

to Axelrod, an organisational Change process is best maneuvered when it involves maximum engagement of its employees. So, while you may have managers or leaders to supervise or steer the Change, it does well to ensure that you secure maximum participation of those who are likely to be most affected by the Change. The more democratic the process, the stronger the foundation on which your new system stands! This may require empowering (Quinn, 1996) the people in the lower rungs of your hierarchy to take charge of the implementation process. Axelrod suggests that by building communities and connecting people across various functions, the probability of creative and more engaged employee participation can be stepped up.

3. For any Change process to work effectively, employees must buy the Change vision. Often, people may agree with the broad context of introducing a Change, but over time may find it difficult to adapt themselves to Change. This obviously can be detrimental to the organisation's Change efforts. Stanley, Meyer and Topolnytsky (2005) recommend a teaching and learning process to counsel employees and help them to adapt to Change.

4. Sometimes, the organisation structure of a company may be such that it hinders open flow of ideas or candid interaction, both horizontally and vertically. Depending upon the type of organisation, reducing hierarchy and bureaucracy is seen to go a long way in promoting free exchange of ideas and hence lesser bottlenecks in the process.

5. A related point is communication. Open communication generates feedback, well or otherwise, which is vital to evaluate the Change process and Change progress. In this direction, the management is required to communicate to its people not only the vision and the strategy behind the Change, but also technical or functional skills required to survive the Change, through training and development programs.

6. This brings us to another important component of Change programs – namely, training & development. One of the best practice company representatives in a research conducted by the American Productivity and Quality Research indicated that empowering employees with authority and responsibility can produce little effect if they are not carried out in conjunction to training

programs that equip employees with the skills and tolls to implement Change. Education is needed both to inform the employees of the organisational context that necessitates the Change as well as train them in leadership, functional and/or technical roles.

7. It was also found in the above mentioned survey that many best practice companies regularly study employee behavior and attitudes and then make the results of these studies available to the workforce. This helps them monitor the culture and attitudes in their organisation, gauge the Changes in the same and understand any further Changes that may be required.

8. Measurement is another common tool that all best practice organisations seem to use. The progress and status of projects are periodically reviewed, and key stakeholders such as customers and the work force chief are surveyed to understand the progress of Change initiatives and identify key areas of Change. The results are typically shared with the workforce.

9. Many best practices followed by companies were also found to align their Human Resource systems with their

organisational Change goals. For instance, they had redone their appraisal systems, initiated 360 degree feedback, developed career paths and revised their incentive systems so as to address the areas of employee behavior, career progress and personal goals of employees in a Change scenario.

10. Commitment and active participation of leadership and Top Management was also found to be one of the most important driving forces of Change. A best practice followed by organisations covered in the survey indicated that their CEO's actively plan and manage organisational Change.

SKILLS & COMPETENCIES REQUIRED TO OVERCOME RESISTANCE TO CHANGE

The best way to engineer a Change is to include your people in your vision for Change, rather than bringing them into the picture at the implementation stage. It does not take rocket science to understand, that a statement like "How would you like to see your company emerge as the best service provider in the next one year?" can expect to meet a much more inviting response from the employees, rather than an imperative like "I shall expect you to work in such and such manner to bring about so and so Change." The Change may have been decided upon already, most of the time it is. But to include your people, especially those that will in time be most affected by the Change, in your vision and then in the policy making stage, helps them be more intimately associated with it. So, your chances of facing resistance are minimized.

Further, you should also be able to appropriately anticipate the kind of resistance that might arise. We said earlier that resistance could range from passivity to non cooperation to strikes etc. Being able to study employee behavior and gauge the degree or type of resistance you may face helps to prepare for the same in advance.

Next, as a leader, the basic skill that you require to successfully steer a Change initiative is to be sensitive enough to the concerns of your employees. Whenever a Change is initiated, it is done with the best of intentions – either to correct a fault in the system or to better the system. So from your perspective, it is always a healthy decision. Understand that your people may not always think so. Inherently, Change always comes across as a difficult situation, and if workers feel threatened by a Change or expect it to jeopardize their jobs, know that it is only natural for them to think so. Hence, instead of persuading them to come around to your point of view, acknowledge their apprehension. Don't disregard or dismiss their fears as irrational. Rather, be supportive and help them overcome their fears. Sometimes a one-to-one interaction or mentoring sessions may be required for individuals particularly averse to Change. As a next step, explain why the Change is necessary and what benefits it is expected to deliver to your organisation and its people.

Communication is another important skill you need to master to successfully implement a Change initiative. At every stage in the Change process, whether in sharing your vision or need for Change or clarifying roles and expectations or devising an action plan, effective communication plays a key role in ensuring that the desired result is produced. Ensure clarity and objectivity in communication at all stages in the process.

Good planning skills are also a prerequisite to carry out successful Change initiatives. For instance, your initiative must be well planned with respect to your budget, resources, time among other things. Further, you need to adequately plan out your project team and Steering Committee, which will collect the initial data to identify your Change priorities and eventually implement the Change. It is on the findings of this team that your Change plan will be based, and in case the Change is cross functional, it is important that the right people be identified and included in the team. Even if the Change is expected to impact a specific area or department, help from other associated departments may be required to accomplish the Change, and hence people from these areas also need to be included in the steering committee. All this requires rigorous foresight and planning. More importantly, you need to anticipate and plan proper training programs to prepare your people for the forthcoming Change and equip them with the skills, functional and otherwise to operate in the Changed circumstances. Many times a Change occurs, unaccompanied by a Change in the reward system to reinforce the new behavior. A Change in the reward system, reporting relationships or performance appraisal system may also need to be planned out.

APPROACH TO MANAGING ORGANISATIONAL CHANGE

Change in any organisation can occur at three levels – technological, structural and behavioral. However, at any level, it almost invariably creates a stress situation for employees. Various factors such as job security, additional workload, shift in culture and expected behavior etc. can trigger stress in a Change environment. The visible results of Change related stress appear in several forms – from low productivity to absenteeism, low morale, low job satisfaction, communication issues etc. McHugh (1997) opines that stress management should form a part of the Change management process. She suggests that since organisational Changes are accompanied by various stressors, a stress management program must be incorporated as part of Change management.

In case of a technological Change, it is important that proper training programs be designed to equip employees with the necessary skills to cope with the Change. Structural Changes may lead to Change in reporting relationships. Usually, Change in reporting relationships logically derive from a Change in the role performed. Hence, a structural Change can involve a Change in the roles and responsibilities of employees, where some people may have to shoulder additional responsibilities. Normally, for some time during the transition phase, the old and new systems continue to operate parallel to each other, before the new system sets in completely. This phase is difficult for employees, and unless job descriptions and responsibilities are meticulously planned out, it could lead to confusion and negative attitudes towards Change. Hence, Change management requires effective planning on this front.

Some Approaches to Effective Change Management

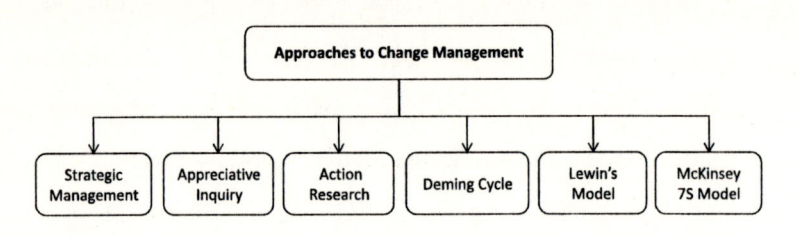

Figure 3.3 – Approaches to Effective Change Management

Strategic Management

Strategic Management is a technique of approaching Change by defining the goal of the Change initiative, then planning the strategy by which that goal is to be realized and formulating indicators that will enable you to understand whether you have reached your goal or not.

Appreciative Inquiry

A recent development in the field of Organisation Design, Appreciative inquiry (AI) asserts that "problems" are only our way of looking at or defining a situation. For instance, a "priority" may be viewed as a "problem" if it is not addressed adequately. Ironically, as long as you consider a priority as a problem, chances are it will restrict your ability to address it appropriately.

Being more of a philosophy than an approach, AI includes within its purview a variety of models, tools and techniques that are offshoots of this philosophy. For instance, one AI approach to strategic planning is to rewind to the best phase or time during the past of the organisation, create a vision of the future and attempt to model methods that worked during the best phase in a way that helps to attain the current vision of the future.

Action Research

Action Research ensures that you proceed with your Change project only after you have taken stock of the current situation. This involves defining an issue and formulating research questions to elucidate or study the same. This is followed by development of a strategy to gather relevant data. The data is then analyzed and an action plan devised accordingly.

PDCA – The Deming Cycle

This initiative is anchored in a very simple self explanatory philosophy - Plan, Do, Check, Act. Developed by Walter Shewhart, it was popularized by Edwards Deming and found initial implementation in the manufacturing industry.

Lewin's Model of Change

Twentieth century psychologist Kurt Lewin describes Change as a three phase cycle comprising the following:

Unfreezing – Every person enjoys a condition, where he can wield some control over his situation and where he feels safe and secure. A Change threatens this stasis, and therefore makes it difficult to unfreeze the individual.

Transition – This phase is marked by the journey that a Change warrants. More often than not, a Change is not one big leap, but a gradual transition into a set of new circumstances.

Re-Freezing – This finally involves creation of a new stasis situation, whereby the Change has been absorbed, and a new stability established.

McKinsey 7S Model

Developed in the late twentieth century, by Tom Peters and Robert Waterman, of McKinsey & Company consulting firm, the McKinsey 7S Model defines seven internal aspects of an organisation and argues that for any company to be successful, these seven factors must exist in mutual cohesion. They include: "Hard" Elements: Strategy, Structure, Systems "Soft"

Elements: Shared Values, Skills, Style, Staff While the "hard" elements may be easier to define, the "soft" elements are less tangible and more closely connected to work culture and ethics. According to the 7S model, irrespective of the type and extent of Change, these 7 elements must be aligned and mutually reinforcing for the Change to successfully endure.

THE CEO AND CHANGE

Given the right circumstances, from no more than dreams, determination, and the liberty to try, quite ordinary people consistently do extraordinary things.

— Dee Hock, founder of VISA International

With all his authority, knowledge and experience, the CEO can empower his people to become incubators of Change rather than only instruments of it. Indeed, by creating the right circumstances, by preparing his people to accept and face Change, and by allowing them to ideate and experiment, the CEO can make a huge difference to the organisation. Interestingly, every individual and by extension every organisation has a lot of hidden potential. The power lies in the CEO to realize and unlock that which is hidden. Further, in instances where a Change is necessitated by an external force, the role of the CEO becomes as important in anticipating and identifying the forces of Change and adapting himself and his organisation accordingly.

A very valuable learning that I took from my first boss was this - You may disagree with an idea because you see a genuine reason for opposing it. But when that idea comes from one senior to you, think awhile. For the mind that gave birth to it was cultured by many years of experience. It is as simple as saying that you disagree with me, because you can see only as far as that first step on the gallery, where you're sitting, allows you to. Ah! If only you would come up to me, and witness the same thing from the last step on the gallery, might you be able to see what I can.... and perhaps then, you would agree!

That is the depth of experience and the extent of foresight that the CEO carries. And that is what can make all the difference.

CHAPTER 4 /

Role of Top Management in Handling Change

It's not that some people have willpower and some don't. It's that some people are ready to change and others are not.

~ James Gordon, M.D. ~

One year had passed and I-Systems had earned their first substantial project.

More importantly, Phase 1 of the project had brought with it, the promise of a yet bigger Phase 2. The only condition was a sterling performance in Phase 1. The pressure to perform, notwithstanding, his team was already celebrating the prospect. Things were looking up, four new people had been recruited into I-Systems and they had managed to do some good damage control to I-System's once waning reputation.

Marcus sat in a corner of the room. People were drinking and cheering each other. Loud music boomed and Chris danced away to glory. Chris! Marcus's thoughts raced back, to the day they had had that crucial meeting – the meeting that had practically defined the following year.

A lot had transpired between him and his employees, before the deal had finally come through. In the event, though, he had lost a very important person – Joe, his key technical guy! Given his quiet response to the Change proposal on Day One, he would never have imagined that Joe would quit. That day in the meeting, he had managed to win over most of his colleagues, reasoning, cajoling, even manipulating constructively, but Joe was the price he had had to pay.

With his senior most technical guy quitting the show, he had had no option but to take over the technical function as CTO of I-Systems. Kay Gibbons had come onboard – investor and CEO! Kay came with a strong management background and superb administrative skills. Sure enough, he went about his role with utmost poise and élan, but 1 year later Marcus knew that it was not only him, not only Kay, but each of those 9 people, his people, who had collectively brought about this Change. From policy making to redefining reporting relationships, from clarifying expectations and delegating work to driving the Change, from sticking to deadlines and delivering "come what may", to cramming that extra bit into their busy schedule, his people, each one of them had worked laboriously round the clock, like motors fitted into a perpetually running machine.... Marcus smiled.

As Chris waved a "Hi!" at him for the fifth time in the last one hour, Marcus couldn't help but think that despite all his apprehension and conflicts, Chris had probably been the key driver all along!

KEY ROLES DURING CHANGE MANAGEMENT

A Change initiative involves a concerted, consistent effort at various levels. The Top Management and Board of Directors are as important to the process as is the Change agent, the sponsors, the steering committee and the people at large.

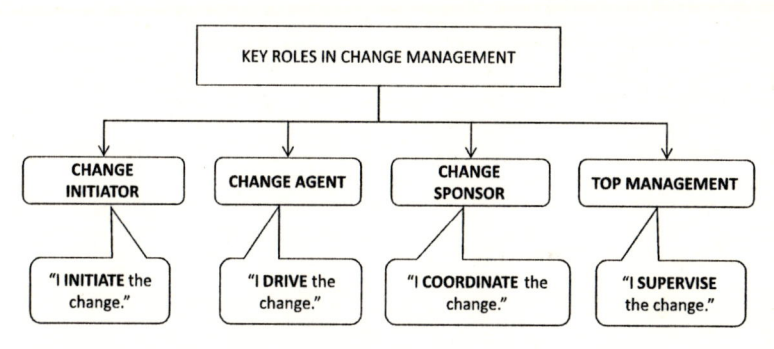

```
                    KEY ROLES IN CHANGE MANAGEMENT
                                 |
        ┌────────────────┬───────┴────────┬────────────────┐
   CHANGE INITIATOR   CHANGE AGENT    CHANGE SPONSOR   TOP MANAGEMENT
        |                |                |                |
  "I INITIATE the   "I DRIVE the    "I COORDINATE the  "I SUPERVISE
     change."         change."          change."        the change."
```

Figure 4.1 – *Key Roles in Change Management*

The various key roles in an organisational Change process include the following:

The Initiator of Change: Organisations often understand the need for Change only when they've been stung by some deep loss. The loss could be in terms of a dipping sales figure, the departure of key people, a fall in the market share or the loss of an important client to a competitor etc. Often, a Change is initiated when someone within the organisation reacts to such events and signals the need for a Change.

The Change Agent: The Change Agent is one who is responsible for driving and implementing Change across the organisation. The Change agent can either be an external consultant or an internal consultant. In fact, at different stages in the Change process, different individuals or teams may come to occupy this role. For instance, if Change management task is outsourced to an external consultant, he serves as the initial Change agent. However, when the project team starts actual work on the recommendations of the consultant, the team leaders become the Change agents. Basically, Change agents at various stages push Change by reinforcing the need to Change, and championing the cause of Change.

The Official Sponsor Team: Usually, the organisation will identify a team or a department to officially coordinate the Change process. In larger organisations, the sponsors may be the HR Department or the IT department. In smaller organisations, a team of senior leaders can play this role.

The Top Management

Finally, while Change efforts are undertaken at the ground level, they need to be steered by the top management. The role of the top management is paramount in ensuring that the initiative does not lose focus or get stranded due to operational or motivational issues.

THE ROLE OF TOP MANAGEMENT

Change can either "make or break" an organisation. Change never takes care of itself. Change is initially difficult but ultimately stabilizes. These are the three basic facts of an organisational Change.

Although after an initial denial phase, people will finally adapt to Change, the transition phase is difficult. And this is where Top Management can help.

As we saw, Change is initiated by one deeply affected by some crisis in the organisation and carried forward by agents and sponsors. However, the success of the Change efforts ultimately rests in the hands of top management. Depending upon the structure of the organisation, the work is delegated to different levels of employee participation depending upon the complexities involved. Thus, the Board of Directors may supervise the CEO, the CEO supervises the Executive Assistants, who in turn delegate work to the middle management, until it trickles down to the entry level supervisors.

The Top Management is instrumental, rather vital in setting the mood for Change. Not only does it play a key role in communicating the vision and the concomitant goals, it also plays a major part in objectively setting targets and defining results to accomplish the Change. People are most deeply influenced by the actions of their supervisors. Hence, leaders themselves need to imbibe the expected behavior that the Change warrants, so as to ensure that they induce such behavior in others.

Top Management Teams can reinforce the agenda for Change by using their power positions or external links, even pushing it through the media, but ultimately, actual progress comes only in collaboration with workers. Again, it is important for top management to generate a sense of collective responsibility. A key to inculcating this attitude lies in genuinely valuing workers and their role in the whole process. There can be nothing more motivating than to know that your labors are acknowledged and appreciated by the company. Adopting a culture that cuts across the hierarchy and treats all people as equals, giving organisational goals priority over personal goals etc. are all perceived as symbolic acts to signify the need for Change and the value that is assigned to it. Thus, a lot lies within the capacity of the top management in terms of sending out the correct signals that will propel Change.

Off late, I noticed that a certain brand of shampoo, has its product (read: the bottle) carry the signature and a small picture of the hair expert they collaborated with to create the product. What are they doing? In my view, they are trying to increase the credibility of the product, so that more people come to trust the brand. Similarly, "selling" a Change to your people requires what I term "credibility management". And that is a major responsibility of the Top Management Team. The top management not only needs to communicate the vision for Change, but also needs to tie the vision to business needs and show how the Change will impact profits, productivity or quality of work life. Equally important is the management's ability to realistically address the existing gap between the current situation and the envisioned situation, and present to the people a powerful, reasonable and well planned strategy – a blueprint for success. Next, driving speedy implementation is extremely important. Once people are convinced of the strategy, the top management needs to quickly put them to "act" upon it. The faster your strategies are put to action, the earlier they are likely to succeed. It's like a "buzzer-round-quiz-game", the faster you hit the buzzer, the more your chances of winning. On the other hand, you may well know the perfect answer, but if you don't hit the buzzer on time, it really doesn't work! Even with a perfect strategy, immediate action becomes the buzzword. With every success you move closer to your vision and increase your credibility, so eventually people will volunteer to follow you.

Another important observation is that during organisational Change, resistance from people is directly proportional to the perceived threat from Change. Change challenges the status quo and demands that people venture out of their comfort zones. It means abandoning the "way things are done" and embracing a new set of potentially better conditions. But despite the potential benefits of Change, it is always initially abominable. It comes with fears of a job loss, a Change in role, a Change in reporting, and so on and so forth till people are so consumed with anxiety and doubt that they have little left to think of it constructively. To maximize benefits from Change, top management must minimize the perceived threats from Change. Many times a lot of the apprehensions may actually be baseless, hence addressing them at the top level means credibly putting unwarranted fears to rest, thereby averting precious loss due to stress and mental anxiety.

So, we spoke of the top management's responsibility in

vision sharing, developing collective responsibility, managing credibility, erasing out meaningless apprehensions, setting goals, defining targets and leading by example, but there's still something we haven't spoken about. Listen, because this is important....

Now consider: How fast did you dismiss the last four words in the preceding paragraph, expecting to stumble upon a great management secret in the next?

Doused expectations apart, the simplest fact that the top management needs to understand about communicating Change is that it is IMPORTANT to LISTEN. Just like most of us would miss the message in those four words, hoping for something greater to follow, the management often skips attention to employee concerns, preferring to advocate rather than to listen. Often, employee concerns can raise relevant issues, which need inclusion in your Change Management Plan. Top Management Teams need to take care, that communication between them and the organisation, is held as interactive sessions, rather than imposing one way talks. Do not rush to explain how great the Change is going to be or offer examples of how people survived earlier Changes and how they were expected to do the same again. Rather, acknowledge that Change is difficult and that every concern is worthy of attention. Be firm on the agenda, but sensitive to the concerns. From there, the secret of effective communication lies in attentive listening, for only when you listen can you respond appropriately. Only when you respond appropriately can you address your people's concerns effectively, and only by doing that can you minimize perceived threats from Change, and maximize productive efforts towards Change. So, take time out, listen and attend to the employees' individual, special needs or issues, while handling Change.

"Selling" Change: A Perspective

Rather than advocating that a certain "new system of working" is better than the "old system of working", Top Management could try the "thesis-antithesis-synthesis" method to communicate Change.

What is meant by "Thesis-Antithesis-Synthesis"?

"Thesis-Antithesis-Synthesis" is a philosophy, commonly associated with the 19th century German thinker, G.W.F. Hegel, who contended that historical evolution is the outcome of conflicting opposites. Simply put, thesis is a statement. Antithesis is the counter statement. Obviously the thesis and the antithesis are contradictory or opposed to each other. The synthesis implies resolving this conflict by offering a solution at a higher level, by combining the positive elements of both the thesis and the antithesis. The synthesis then forms a new thesis, which, in time, encounters an antithesis, and is resolved at the next higher level through another synthesis. This philosophy is often used to explain Hegel's dialectic on the process of historical evolution.

How can it be applied to organisational Change?

In our context, let us take the current situation as the thesis. So, the new system or the ideal situation is the antithesis. Now, if you try to impose that the new system is better than the old because of a, b, c, d, e reasons, you pose a challenge that is most likely to be resisted. No one wants to think that they are operating in a sham system, which is no longer capable of working. Instead, try striking a "synthesis" between the current and the ideal situation. Communicate the positives in the current system and the desirables from the ideal system. Suggest that the Change will bring about a synthesis between the two, for better functioning. This way, you promote the Change, without devaluing the current way of working. Psychologically, this has a positive impact on the way people react to the idea of Change.

Moving ahead, the top management need also ensure that work processes, performance systems, training programs, job descriptions etc. that form or support the framework within which employees work, are aligned to the Change objective and complement each other.

While, in general, Change calls upon identifying the different business units involved and delegating work to them, through able team leaders, the top management needs to chart out a macro plan. Having identified the tasks involved in achieving Change and the time frame available to complete those tasks, top management must map a critical path of all tasks, wherein they have a clear picture of which task has to be completed by when, which task follows which, and how are different task areas tied to each other. This helps achieve synchronization of work efforts, without which the desired Change can never be achieved. From there, the team leaders can take on the responsibility of guiding their respective teams to achieve the set targets within the defined time to accomplish Change.

Various studies in the area have shown that it is a better approach for top management to work its way through the existing culture than trying to Change it, all of a sudden. This can be done through a shared vision and a buy-in of managers operating at the lower levels of hierarchy. Generating an interest among them and the employees they supervise means pulling in precious energy for your project. For, the real work needed to implement your plans happens here. Once they are committed to their roles in achieving Change, the project can pick up considerable speed. However, while the management adopts such an employee oriented approach, it must also ensure that those not committed to their roles be mentored or shown the door.

Research has shown that many companies, for instance, Navistar International Corporation, who spectacularly accomplished Change, did so, not by engaging external consultants, but by having their top management study the organisational context, company history, standard operating procedures and then building improvement teams to drive Change wherever required. Thus, these results sufficiently testify to the importance of the Top Management Teams' role in handling organisational Change.

PARTICIPATION OF BOARD OF DIRECTORS IN THE PROCESS OF CHANGE

Organisation wide Change calls for the active participation of the Board of Directors. The involvement may be core or superficial, depending upon the complexity and urgency of the project, but having the Board as part of the team helps to drive the project in the right direction.

The Board exercises full authority over allocation of resources. So, the manner or extent to which the Board makes money, people, time and other resources available to you is a measure of the importance they attach to your moves. "Power Play" may sound like a repulsive word to many, but in the context of an organisations Change, it demands attention. The Board ensures political support for Change, which can step up the existing motivation and speed levels for Change. If the Board supports your Change project, there is higher chance that motivation levels and speed at work will be affected positively. Hence, it is a good idea to have the Board formally approve of the project as well as the Change Management Plan before embarking on it. Involvement of Board Members in the project may also open up other strategic areas that require Change, for the outcome of the current Change project to be visible. This is because the Board has a much more panoramic view of the organisation's current standing than the team leaders or employees. Hence, ground level research and data support from the project teams may enable them to identify multiple related issues that need to be addressed to successfully maneuver the Change. To this extent, having a Board member to oversee the work of the project team at the data collection and analysis phase can actually serve as a leverage point. Including Board Development as a part of the Change Strategy may be a good way of ensuring Board Support to the Change project.

The Board can be a very valuable guide in the development and implementation of action plans. With their knowledge and experience, they can also make useful contribution to planning, leading, supervising and managing the project. Their problem solving skills could also come in handy to tackle tricky Change situations.

The Board can also offer objective review and evaluation of Project Goals and Results. Further, if for some reason, the project is stalled to address a more urgent issue, the Board can be of help while reviving the project. Hence it is advisable that at least one Board Member be included on the Project Team, to ensure that the project progresses in the desired direction rather than losing focus midway and dissipating.

Naturally then, it is also important that in order to enable the Board guide the Change project properly, the findings of the Project Team, in Phase II of the project is communicated to them. Regular updates on the progress of the project also need to be shared with the Board, for best results.

THE IMPORTANCE OF PLAYING FACILITATOR, COACH AND TRAINER

Whether you happen to be an external or an internal consultant, as a Change agent, you need to juggle the roles of facilitating, coaching and training your client. More importantly, you will need to identify when to carry out which role. Initially, you will probably be required to don the role of a facilitator. In this role, your main objective is to help your client decide on the type of Change he wants, how he may achieve that Change and finally help him to bring about that Change. As a Change agent, you will have to encourage your client or your client group to come out with diverse perspectives and aspects of the Change situation, to understand where precisely to direct your energies. Also, take care to ensure that the beliefs and opinions of all members present are solicited, valued and incorporate in an appropriate manner, while addressing the questions what to achieve and how to achieve.

Quite often, individuals in your team might not be able to

overcome resistance to Change. Alternatively, while some may be open to the idea of Change, they may not be clear on their precise role in the Change. Yet others may find it difficult to adapt to a Change. These are times when you will need to coach your client's team to push the Change forward.

Observe whether the team requires any specialized knowledge like conducting a market research etc. to carry out their roles. Often, more generalised knowledge such as that of performance management or financial systems etc. might be required. You might then take on the role of Trainer or if need be, facilitate appropriate training and development programs.

MANAGING CHANGE SUCCESSFULLY – HOW CAN CEO'S ACHIEVE THIS?

In a survey conducted by the American Productivity and Quality Centre, researchers indicated that since Change is almost always met by resistance, there arises the need for a champion to drive Change across the organisation. Further the more powerful and visible the champion is, the more successful the Change project tends to be. In this direction, the research concluded that the leader of the organisation, most often the CEO is often the most effective communicator of the vision and the necessity of Change across the organisation. In fact, Change projects in most of the best practice organisations were found to be spearheaded, planned and managed by the CEO of the Company.

Often, it is not enough for the CEO to just communicate the vision to the workforce. In order to ensure that vision successfully translates into reality, the CEO must also play a major role in planning and implementing the Change process. The active involvement of the CEO in the project underlines the significance of the same, thus ensuring organisation wide support and commitment.

The CEO Perspective

Often times, Change is viewed as an objectively measurable output. It could be a surge in sales figures, a new business unit or a process reengineering. However, what some CEO's may miss is the transition phase. Till the output becomes visible and operating, the impression could be that the Change effort has been unsuccessful or worst not achieved. Fact is, the transition phase, which precedes the phase where Change results become visible is not only the toughest phase, but is also the phase where the maximum Change effort is required. This is a time, when people are adapting to the new situation, adjusting themselves into new found responsibilities, and sometimes operating both old and new systems simultaneously. While this phase may not show any visible output, this is the phase where the maximum Change is actually taking place. The CEO needs to empathize with his employees during this phase rather than worry about the observable result. The only hurdle that they may face is there are no limits to how long a transition phase will last before the Change finally sets in and becomes visible.

Another hurdle for the CEO is to effectively handle pressure situations, wherein the Board may want to see how the Change has affected a return on investment too soon. This disregards the fact that a Change is always gradual and can eventually lead to a regression.

A third challenge, which is quite inconspicuous, is that the CEO often runs a shorter transition cycle than the middle management, and hence is actually not as "connected" to the middle management as he may feel. The reason is that, for him, the Change is often signified by the accomplishment of a strategic objective, whereas for the middle management, the actual Change impact sets in after the objective has been achieved and a new set of circumstances established. For it is the middle management that has to deal with this Change on a daily basis, slowly regularising the Change to make it a part of the system. That requires time. Hence, a longer transition phase. This disconnect, between the CEO and the middle management in a Change scenario can pose a challenge to the CEO.

In a McKinsey Quarterly, Carolyn B Aiken and Scott P Keller opined that, the precise nature of challenge facing the CEO can never be foretold. Rather, it varies with the size, urgency and nature of the transition undertaken; the strengths and weaknesses of the organisation; and the personal qualities of the leader.

However, in general, they identified four pointers that define the CEO's role in a Change initiative. They are:

A. A realistic, meaningful vision: Most people work best for a cause that they can believe in. The power to inspire valuable Change efforts rests, in the first instance, on the CEO's rendering of a powerful transformation story. The more personally he can engage people in his vision and the more actively he can assure people of the value add that comes with the Change, the more successful the effort will turn out to be. Also, people gain a lot more confidence in the Change proposal, when their several apprehensions are addressed personally by the CEO. It goes a long way in securing their commitment by restoring the security which the change generally threatens..

B. "Walking the Talk": The CEO, can inspire his organisation by role modelling expected behaviours. Indeed the CEO is expected to be the Change he wants to see. Naranyana Murthy's decision to take on the role of 'chief mentor' at Infosys in 2002, had a far-reaching impact on his role as the CEO of the Company. For it meant that, with this new engagement, he would have to step out of many formal responsibilities that he would otherwise have performed. But the commitment in his decision strikes you as extraordinary - "You have to sacrifice yourself for a big cause before you can ask others to do the same," he says. "A good leader knows how to retreat into the background gracefully while encouraging his successor to be more and more successful in the job."

C. A secure and dedicated Project team: Setting up a secure and dedicated top team requires considerable effort from the CEO, to identify people with the drive and the ability to steer the Change. In this direction, it was found that a matrix with "business performance" on one axis and "role-modelling desired behaviour" on the other can help zero in on the right talents. Those who display the desired behaviour and high performance are capable of pushing Change, while those showing undesired behaviour and low performance need mentoring and coaching.

D. The Personal Touch: Nothing can beat personal involvement of the CEO in driving Change. In fact, the impact on the teams morale and efforts to successfully achieve change is a lasting one when the CEO goes out of the way to dedicate himself to operational difficulties at hand. Does Marcus's situation, described at the beginning of this chapter, ring a bell?

CHAPTER 5 /

Types of Management Strategies in Handling Change

Everyone thinks of changing the world, but no one thinks of changing himself.

~ *Leo Tolstoy* ~

Phase 2 was, indeed, much bigger than Phase 1. And Marcus knew intuitively that taking it up, would require some major Changes to the organisational structure and "the way they did things there". No more of Genevieve shuttling roles between different functions, can't have Chris do that either. They must concentrate on one and only one area.

His new recruits had picked up quite a lot of work, so Genevieve, Chris, Martha and Cathy could stop donning different roles and assume more defined responsibilities...The dotted line reporting to Kay was also an added burden, but could they do anything about that? Marcus did a quick mental calculation.

9+4=13. Yes, 13....that was his current people strength, excluding Kay and himself that is.

Ummm... It would do good to compartmentalize his people, he thought. Maybe, we could have...how many... three groups? ... And...and...But he could think no more. It had been a hectic day at work and tomorrow would only be tougher. A little sleep was the least he could gift himself!

"How about a Business Analysis Group, a Technical Group and a Quality Assurance team? Each group takes charge of its own area, and each group has a team leader to oversee progress. Any

suggestions?" Marcus asked at the meeting, he had called to discuss "an urgent makeover". Yes! That is what his mail had said...

"And who do the team leads report to?" Chris asked.

"They can have a functional reporting with me and an administrative reporting with Kay."

"The only issue would be that given the short time we have to complete this phase, the weekly review meets may lead to unnecessary delays. Why not have the teams lead take stock of regular progress, and retain just a functional reporting with you?"

Marcus looked at Kay. "A difficult one Chris had tossed this time....He knew Chris was right! But how would Kay react?" he thought.

To his surprise, Kay seemed OK with it, "given the circumstances". In a very subtle way, Chris had helped him address the need of the hour, while bringing back the comfort and rapport of the good old days!!With his key people reporting to him, Marcus was now confident that they could make this project a huge success...After all his biggest strength, his people, were back with him again!!

What Marcus did was to build a strategy to tackle the Change ahead. Theoretically, there are various strategies that explain how Change can be successfully initiated and implemented. However, before we move on to those, let us take a look at some of the common things to consider, before you embark upon an organisational Change:

1. What do I want to Change? Typically this might point towards a specific "problem" area.

2. Is this the fundamental thing that needs to Change or is there a deeper "reason" lurking behind the "problem" that needs to be addressed? This question is particularly important because many times, after the Change process has been run halfway, it is realized that a problem exists at a more basic level. Focus then shifts between new Change areas that are discovered and the energy of Change efforts get dissipated.

3. Why do I want the Change?

4. How will I achieve the Change? This will involve weighing the risk and incentives, balancing them out and addressing

any gaps between intended process to achieve the Change and issues related to these processes.

5. What about the finances required in implementing the Change?

6. Will business possibly continue as usual during the Change phase or will it get affected adversely?

7. What type of resource (external or internal consultants) should I use, given the size of my organisation and knowledge base?

8. How, if at all, will the Change impact the work culture or vice versa?

9. How critical is the situation and how much time do I have to respond to it?

10. Does my core Change driver team have the contextual and operational knowledge, capability and influence to survive the Change process or do I need to empower them in some way?

CHANGE MANAGEMENT STRATEGIES

Once you have precise answers to these elementary questions, you can decide upon the strategy you want to adopt. Theory offers at least four different Change strategies. In practice, we typically use a combination of some or all of these to address Change situations. These four strategies are: The Empirical-Rational Approach, the Normative-Reeducative Approach, the Power-Coercive Approach and the Environmental-Adaptive Approach.

All four provide you with different insights into the type of Change environment that may exist in an organisation. The type of Change environment broadly varies with the ideology of the informal organisation or the cultural consensus that they may share and the type of Change being introduced. The relevance of the different Change strategies lies in the fact that they explore different assumptions about human motivation and behavior in order to understand or anticipate response to Change. Thus, they take into account the psychology of the informal organisation, and hence help effectively manage the human side of Change.

Their beauty, however, is that they are never mutually exclusive, and different strategies may be used at different stages in the Change process. Thus, depending on your Change environment, you must decide on the appropriate mix of strategies, to be used to push Change.

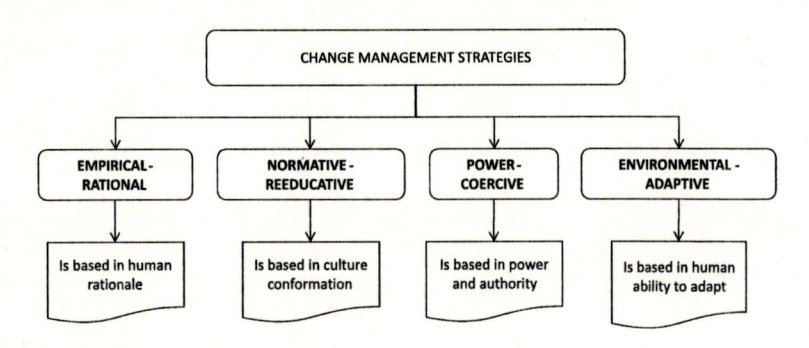

```
                    CHANGE MANAGEMENT STRATEGIES
                                 |
        ┌────────────────┬───────┴────────┬────────────────┐
   EMPIRICAL-       NORMATIVE-        POWER-         ENVIRONMENTAL-
   RATIONAL         REEDUCATIVE       COERCIVE       ADAPTIVE
        |                |                |                |
   Is based in      Is based in       Is based in      Is based in
   human            culture           power and        human ability
   rationale        conformation      authority        to adapt
```

Figure 5.1 – Change Management Strategies

EMPIRICAL-RATIONAL STRATEGY

A "classic" approach to Change management, developed by Robert Chin and Kenneth D. Benne, this strategy is built on the premise that, in general, human beings are rational and can be reasoned with.

Hence, although Change innately is resisted, people can be won over by –

1) The genuine logic behind the Change, and
2) By what is there in it for *them*.

If people are convinced on these two aspects of change, the process becomes easily navigable. Thus, this strategy uses persuasion to make individuals accede to Change, through planned, managed dissemination of information, which makes the incentives of Change clear to them. Thus, this strategy demands skilful use of communication in selling the benefits of Change. The emphasis is on providing correct information, education and training that inspire people to Change of their own volition. Also, it is important to identify potential carriers of Change — people who willingly accept the Change, and are influential enough to spread the same.

The role of the CEO is important here. Being the leader of the organisation, not only is he an influential figure, but also has relatively more credibility than anyone else in the organisation. Hence, he can play a major role in securing the buy-in of his people and inspiring them to embrace the Change.

However, by virtue of rationale again, people are seen to be generally resistant to Change, if it has an imbedded downside that is not balanced or offset by an equal upside. Hence, a foolproof plan for successfully initiating Change, or at least managing the human side of it, must work out the following:

- A strong basis for initiating the Change

- Linkage to actual benefits or incentives to be derived from the Change

- The pros and cons, including an exercise on possible measures to negate the "cons"

This strategy works well only if you can balance the incentives against the risks in a profitable manner i.e. only if you are able to show that the value-add from the Change is proportionately much higher than the risk involved.

This strategy becomes difficult to execute, if your risks outweigh your incentives, and especially so, if the general perception is that your company is in a relatively comfortable position, even without the Change. A good idea then might be to show people some genuine reasons as to why the perceived comfort is just a passing phase and won't last long.

In such a situation, some people may buy your logic, some may not. If you find the buyers to be capable of influencing the rest, endeavor to form a class that can serve as interpreters between you and the mass of people, and hence serve as drivers of Change.

For the empirical-rational approach to succeed in the later phases of Change, you also need to build your case on a strong Current Situation Analysis, proceed with proper training and development programs, initiate appropriate education, and carry out relevant research and development to support the Change. Hire the services of field experts and Organisational Design and Change specialists if required. Once these backups are in place, people will inevitably become much more confident of shouldering the responsibilities of Change. Also, while you may initially identify a representative class to drive the Change, eventually you must graduate to a phase where every team player is encouraged to come up with creative solutions aligned towards attaining a "best-of-all" situation.

However, the Empirical Rational Approach disregards the fact that while employees may understand the need for Change or the rationale behind Change, they may still not like to undergo Change, because of the emotional troubles, adjustment issues etc. that come with transition.

NORMATIVE – RE-EDUCATIVE STRATEGY

Another "classic" approach to Change management, this strategy takes wings from the fact that humans are social beings. Hence, they always have the inherent urge to conform to social norms and standards.

It does not deny that humans are rational and intelligent creatures, but views their behavior as being guided by socio-cultural norms and their allegiance to these norms. Change is introduced by restructuring their normative orientations and inducing them to commit to new norms.

Often, a cultural shift in the organisation becomes imperative to adapt to market situations and survive competition. For example, your competitor may be producing twice your output because of their technological advancement, whereas you lag behind because you still rely on manual operations. This needs you to shift work culture from a manual to a technology oriented people set, which in turn requires you to appropriately train and prepare people for the Change. Normative – Reeducative Strategy is defined as a strategy that believes that norms in an organisation can be purposely shifted to attain higher productivity, through collective people efforts.

Given that culture and norms quickly become a part of who you are, an initial resistance to anything non conformist or maverick is quite expected. Ironically, norms and standards too are not constant over time. If they had been, evolution of society would never have been possible. Just like a stream of water that Changes its course, when it meets a strong obstruction, culture and norms can also be re-established and redefined.

This approach believes that changing the attitudes, values and culture leads to an automatic Change in behavior. The very logic that makes initial resistance to such Change inevitable is used to explain how, over a period of time, this kind of a Change tends to adhere. Thus, although it may be paradoxical, it is actually practically observable that once a new culture sets in, people instinctively feel the need to conform, simply in order to survive.

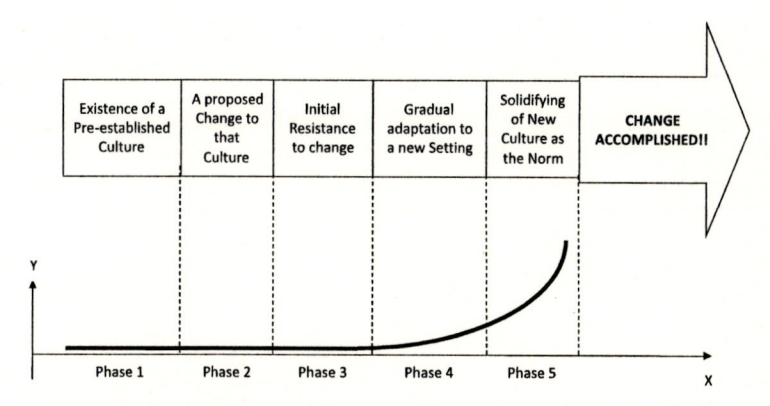

Existence of a Pre-established Culture	A proposed Change to that Culture	Initial Resistance to change	Gradual adaptation to a new Setting	Solidifying of New Culture as the Norm	CHANGE ACCOMPLISHED!!
Phase 1	Phase 2	Phase 3	Phase 4	Phase 5	

Figure 5.2 - Phases in the Implementation of Normative-Reeducative Strategy

X axis shows Phases in the Implementation of Normative-Reeducative Strategy
Y axis shows the Acceptance Levels for the new culture corresponding to each phase

An important tool in initiating this Change is the presence of a magnetic and dynamic personality, who can considerably influence people and their perspectives. This personality can be a leader, a Change agent or most effectively, the CEO of the company. Given his visibility, prominence, credibility and authority in an organisation, he possesses all that is required to effect a Change.

While a culture Change is possible, it is never immediate. For it implies considerable adjustments to the hitherto established thought patterns and mindsets. As a result, it can emerge only as an outcome of a gradual process. Hence, this strategy is applicable only if you have a longer time frame at your disposal for enabling the Change.

The Normative – Reeducative Approach is perhaps the most widely used strategy in present times. When using this strategy, it is important to remember that it is better to try and work through the existing culture, collaborating with people, and helping them see a new and better possibility, than to wake up one fine morning and replace it with a new culture. After all, you cannot Change culture the way you change clothes, because it connects to a deeper part of you and how you operate. So, this approach calls for an honest endeavor to work in sync with people, identify problems and facilitate solutions. It should be directed towards improving problem-solving capacities, upgrading processes within a system, and fostering new attitudes, skills, and norms for people. While the bright side is that when your efforts engage people so much, chances of resistance are minimized. But on the other side of the coin, this approach is too dependent on employee cooperation. For instance, new software developed for a certain insurance company was found to be left unused even till months after, because the employees did not want to step out of the comfort of the "old way of doing things." Often, such a Change involves unlearning and relearning, and while the Change may ultimately trigger simpler solutions to their work problems, the transition phase comes as a real challenge, often leading to resistance.

This strategy could be used in conjunction with a Change in the employee performance management systems that reward people who facilitate Change and penalize those who oppose it. This may help to beat the resistance and build a more cooperative atmosphere. Further, since work culture falls as much within the domains of the formal organisation as the informal organisation. Therefore, a Change to the work culture can succeed only if an amiable relationship exists between these two counterparts, or at least if leaders of the informal organisation buy the proposed Change.

Another perspective on this strategy tells us that while most of the time, individuals prefer to stick to established conventions, the story is different when people within the system are not happy with the status quo. This is a situation where people are actually looking out for Change. In this scenario, the preliminary step that the management needs to take to trigger a Change is to evaluate and clarify organisational norms and culture. This can be done through interactions, discussions and at a personal level, introspection by the employees of the organisation. So, more often, this strategy will intimately involve people in the "process" of Change rather than have them face only the "impact"of Change.

Hence, the normative-reeducative approach targets attitudes and values. It tends to produce long lasting changes as it usually involves group goals, group norms or common values. The reason is that once a new norm sets in, after being initiated either by the formal or the informal organisation, it eventually becomes part of the system – "the way things are" - and therefore stabilizes over time.

POWER – COERCIVE STRATEGY

This "classic" strategy bases itself in the power of "power". According to Hans Morgenthau:

Power may comprise anything that establishes and maintains the control of man over man. Thus power covers all social relationships, which serve that end, from physical violence to the most subtle psychological ties by which one mind controls another.

Applied to our context, this strategy advocates "power" in the form of threat sanctions, and believes that people are, in general compliant, and will ultimately bow down to those who possess greater power.

At times, when the Change is not radical but moderate, the company may also use subtler forms of power or hegemonic power to attain its objective. In fact, the Normative Reeducative Approach or the Empirical Rational Approach ultimately uses hegemonic power very subtly, to navigate through the Change process. Hegemony is like an internalized form of social control which makes us feel we are choosing when really we have no choice. The 20th century French Marxist Louis Althusser called this 'trick' as Interpellation.

In both these cases, when a Change has been decided upon, people have no choice but to accept it. They may resist for some time, but ultimately must go with the flow. However, instead of using force, these strategies use "reason" and "collaboration" to make the "Change situation" seem like a choice that will lead to a better situation than the status quo. So, while the idea that the Change will lead to a prospective better situation is true, it is ultimately never open to choice. Hence, indirectly even these strategies use some form of subtler hegemonic power. However, the difference is that while these approaches secure the support of the people through logic or collaboration, hence ensuring that Change endures and stabilizes over time, the direct use of imposing power, as advocated by the Power – Coercive Strategy, runs the risk that once the power is removed, people may revert to their original behavior.

But many times, exerting authority, subtly or otherwise, in the form of political and economic sanctions, legislation, policies, "moral" power etc. may seem the only way to bring about a Change. This happens when people in the organisation collectively fail to perceive a threat that is, in reality, grave and must be resolved within a restricted response time. Use of power may also be necessary when people become obstinate and intractable in the face of a Change, which has lots at stake. So, people may become even during times of an exigency. The trick applied here is to have it your way and leave no other option for your people but to accept the Change. While political sanctions usually reward non conformists with imprisonment, economic sanctions curtail financial incentives to those who resist the Change. Thus, the use of coercive power is an attempt to make people yield to Change by inducing fear or using actual force.

However, the use of power may not always be negative. For instance, one power – coercive strategy uses the behavioral psychology concept of "the carrot and the stick". In this approach, power can be used to both reward employees who support Change through financial incentives and punish those who don't with political or financial consequences, through sanctions. Thus, power can operate both ways.

The success of this strategy, however, depends on the general temperament of the organisation.

Some organisations, as a part of their culture, believe in the authority of seniority, and appreciate the role of the hierarchy in issuing guidelines or directives for organisational development. If your people are attuned to a system of healthy authoritarianism, this may come easy. But in an organisation where liberality has long been practiced, Hitlerian tactics will face resistance. Still, with Power-Coercive strategies, people have little option but to accept Change, since most of these strategies use stringent policies, where impunity is ruled out. However, to ensure that the foundations of Change are built on unanimity rather than repressed fear or dissatisfaction, it is important to evaluate the nature of your organisation, the problem at hand and the time frame at hand, before embarking on this strategy, as a last resort.

Robert L. Kahn observed that:

To say that A has the power to Change B's behavior necessarily implies that A exerts some force in opposition to some or all of the previously existing forces [including B's own needs and values] on B. This is conflict....The exercise of [coercive] power, thus, necessarily creates conflict...

Thus, while the use of authority structures and threat sanctions can accomplish Change, they may breed hatred and contempt for the organisation or the senior management, which is harmful to organisation in the long run.

ENVIRONMENTAL – ADAPTIVE STRATEGY

The Environmental-Adaptive Strategy, suggested by Fred Nickols, is built on the premise that while people innately resist Change, they also eventually adapt themselves to it, when they are left with no choice.

Also known as the "die – on – the – vine" strategy, it takes its cue from the common observation that while individuals are quick to oppose Change that they find threatening, they also have an innate ability to adapt quickly to a new set of circumstances. Applied to our context of organisational Change, this human psychology translates to a strategy of first creating a new environment and then gradually moving people from the old to the new system. Thus, rather than proactively trying to "Change" the organisation by effecting a "Change" in the behavior, processes, culture and norms of people, this strategy recommends that a new set of circumstances be created, and the innate nature of humans to eventually adapt be exploited, in letting the Change "sink in". Therefore, in this strategy, the ball shifts court from the management to the people, as the responsibility of regularizing the Change now lies on the people and how they adapt to the Change. They practically have no choice to accept or reject the Change, unless of course one prefers to quit the organisation altogether. Here, the Change is made, and the individuals merely adapt themselves.

This strategy is best suited for Changes that are radical in nature rather than those that are gradual. Say, you want to introduce the SAP-HR system to increase efficiency and speed of HR related work. This is an incremental Change that will happen over time, as your Business HR personnel gradually learn how to operate the new system and shift from the old manual practice to the new systematized process. If you were to use the Environment Adaptive strategy here, creating the environment and leaving them to adapt to it in their own way, the transition phase, very likely would stretch too long. This is because, your managers already operate within a framework that they are comfortable with, and so they may be reluctant to shift to a new system. Here, you might have to use a mix of the empirical-rational and the normative-reeducative strategies instead to Change that comfort culture and enable them embrace the Change.

Now, consider the example that Nickols gives, of a radical Change handled in the Environmental-Adaptive way. Rupert Murdoch wanted to shift to an entirely new operating structure, on terms that were very different from the current one at Fleet Street. So, he set about quietly establishing an entirely new operation in Wapping, some distance away from Fleet Street. As soon as the new system became operational, he informed the printers at Fleet Street that he had some good news and some bad news for all of them. The bad news was that they would have to shut down their operations at Fleet Street. So, everybody was fired. The good news was that a new operation had jobs for all of them, albeit on very different terms.

Now, most people in this situation will embrace the new option – a radical Change, tackled using the Environment-Adaptive strategy. Of course, the strategy is a mix of the empirical rational and power coercive strategies, and that is only a reinforcement of the fact that practical situations often need a mix of different strategies to effectively manage Change.

Many years ago, my work took me to a slum infested area. I was pained to see the kind of life those people led, the abject poverty everywhere, the bowl that every child held out in his hand, not for food, but in the hope that a kind passerby may drop some alms.

A few weeks ago, I got the opportunity of revisiting the same place to run an education camp, and was pleasantly amazed at the buildings that stood in place of the slums – an obvious outcome of a rigorous rehabilitation program! It was only when I ventured inside that I realized, that barring the safer, better and more decent dwelling place to live in, nothing much had really changed. The litter was still around, the kids still ran about in the mud in tattered clothes and they still held out their hands for alms. The rehabilitation program had done well in shifting them to a new place, but perhaps something more remained to be done to have them live a new, more meaningful life. Their "homes" had changed, their way of life hadn't.

And to Change that culture, they needed to be educated, to be shown that a better way of life existed, and existed within their reach. But even for that education to show its impact, I was now beginning to understand, I needed more kids like Jana, Neil and Don. Among the close to thirty kids I had been asked to supervise, there were only these three who were genuinely interested. The rest were happy with their life, as it was.

The above incident links to an important factor that you must consider before using this strategy. Ensure that you have at least a few capable, influential and probably "non conformist" employees, in your organisation, who will embrace the Change and drive the others. These are your "seed" employees – people who will foster a new and more effective work culture in the newly established setup. Correspondingly, Nickols uses the term "bad apples" to refer to people from the old culture, which are detrimental to the new culture and must be done away with.

If there is no buy-in on the Change, at-least at the "seed" level, the strategy may not work. Rather, it may lead to a situation where you have a new workplace that continues to work in the old manner and follow the old culture. Effectively then, there hasn't been much Change.

HOW DO I SELECT THE RIGHT STRATEGY?

While, in practice, you will probably require a mix of strategies, a few "Things to Remember" can help you choose the right mix of strategy that fits your situation.

For instance, if the Change is radical, it is best to go for an environmental adaptive strategy. In incremental Changes, a mix of the other strategies can be used. Further, in case of a more or less submissive organisation, empirical rational or normative re-educative strategies work well. However, if you anticipate strong opposition, the "n" power coercive is the way to go.

A diverse population requires a mix of different strategies. A shorter time frame warrants the use of power coercive strategy, but when you have a relaxed time frame, you can again use a mix of strategies. Again, if the stakes are high, you may have to use power coercive strategies as the only option, since you cannot leave much to chance. However, in moderate or low stake situations, avoid using power coercive techniques. A diverse population requires a mix of different strategies. Non availability of area experts may leave power coercive strategy as the only option, whereas, availability of expertise allows a mix of other strategies.

Finally, we can say that there is no standard strategy that works for all or most Change situations. Rather, every Change situation is unique in it, and involves unique triggers, cultures, population, resistance, scale etc. However, knowledge of different Change strategies, combined with an understanding of when to use them can help you decide on the correct mix of strategies for your purpose. That said, for Change to succeed, it is important to develop a "critical mass" of individuals who can think creatively and initiate positive Change in the organisation proactively. Also, when a Change is announced, identify individuals who willingly adopt the Change and can create a ripple effect in the organisation.

CHAPTER 6 /

Role of Top Management in Communicating Organisational Change

The most important thing in communication is hearing what isn't said.

~ Peter Drucker ~

SIGNIFICANCE OF COMMUNICATING CHANGE

In a survey conducted across 198 companies, spanning The United States, Great Britain and Japan, Blake and Mouton stumbled upon "Communication" as the most prominent roadblock to achieving corporate excellence (1968). Several years down the line, this still holds true.

Organisational Change seldom comes easy, and communication skills are perhaps the most important quality required to overcome resistance to Change. An organisational Change calls for effective communication at various stages. From communicating the vision for Change to explaining the need to Change, from inspiring people to participate in the Change to clarifying their roles and expectations, from handling resistance to Change to educating and training them, from preparing people for the Change to equipping them with the desired skills to face the Change, in each and every step of your Change process, communication plays a key role.

FACTORS INVOLVED IN COMMUNICATING CHANGE

```
┌─────────────────────────┬─────────────────────────┐
│                         │                         │
│    Right Content        │    Right Communicator   │
│              ┌──────────────────────┐             │
│              │      Effective       │             │
│              │    Communication     │             │
│              └──────────────────────┘             │
│    Right Channel        │    Right Time           │
│                         │                         │
└─────────────────────────┴─────────────────────────┘
```

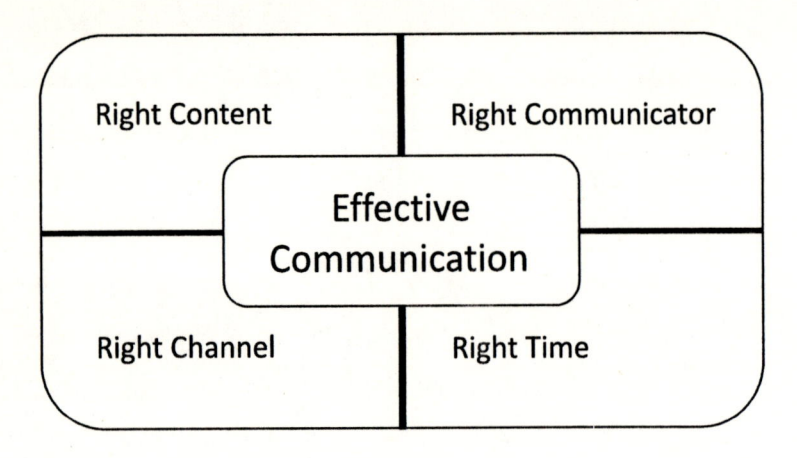

Figure 6.1 – Factors involved in communicating Change

The figure above summarises the four basic requirements of an effective piece of communication – right message, right sender, correct timing and an appropriate channel. It is as important to structure the right content of your communication plan as it is to decide who would be the right person to communicate the Change. Properly timing your communication and releasing the information through an effective medium, for instance, through an email or at a face-to-face meet also has considerable impact on the way people respond to it. Some other factors involved in communicating Change include the following:

1. In the context of an organisational Change, the content of your communication is extremely important. Many companies fail to succeed in their Change efforts, because they often do not communicate a sensible vision for Change, which is inspiring or credible enough.

2. Secondly, "how" you communicate is just as important as "what" you communicate. In fact, one of the most important aspects of communicating a Change is to ensure that your message communicates exactly what you intend to convey. Many times, hidden implications may lead people to misinterpret communication leading to a faulty response. Just like many literary theories suggest that the meaning of a book lies in the reader rather than the writer, so does the meaning of a communication lie in the receiver or the perceiver, rather than the sender. Hence, rather than the sender's intent, it is the receiver's response to the communication that actually indicates the meaning of the communication. There may be various "interpretive communities" within your informal organisation i.e. different groups of people may interpret the same message in different ways, depending upon their own ideologies or thought patterns. Make your communication, simple,

straight, clear and precise to avoid misinterpretation and misunderstanding.

3. Communication involves gauging the values and intentions of your customers and employees as much as knowing your own intentions, and effective communication requires aligning the latter to the former. Since, as we saw earlier, meaning resides in the receiver (in case of an organisation, your employees and customers) rather than the sender, knowing their intentions and aligning your message with the same, improves the impact of communication.

4. Always lend a "human touch" to all your communication, genuinely. Remember that your organisation function through people and for people. In any communication, make them feel respected and valued. At a deeper level, it means that the Change you communicate also adequately takes into account your people and not only your profits.

5. The impact of communication also depends, to a great extent, on the rapport between the sender and the receiver. Amiable working relationships between the employees and the top management automatically ensure that your people are more receptive to your ideas.

COMMUNICATING CHANGE: KOTTER'S PERSPECTIVE

Kotter extends seven principles of effective communication, shown in the diagram.

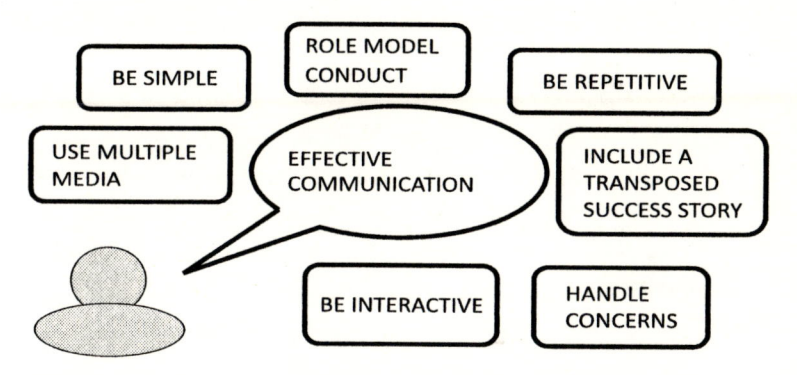

```
      BE SIMPLE     ROLE MODEL        BE REPETITIVE
                     CONDUCT
   USE MULTIPLE    EFFECTIVE         INCLUDE A
      MEDIA      COMMUNICATION      TRANSPOSED
                                   SUCCESS STORY

                  BE INTERACTIVE      HANDLE
                                     CONCERNS
```

Figure 6.2 - Kotter's building blocks for a powerful Change communication

- *Simplicity* – The simpler the message, the lesser the chance of miscommunication. Consciously avoid technical jargon, and keep your message as uncomplicated as possible.

- *Transposing your Success Story* – Nothing works like a success story. Especially, if you occupy a leadership position, link your personal experience or success story to the proposed Change to paint a powerful vision.

- *Multiple Media* – Use different media of communication such as the internet, intranet, emails, face-to-face interactions, newsletters etc. to reach out to the mass of people.

- *Repetitions* – An idea, when repeated again and again, compels attention.

- *Role Modelling Behaviour* – Only when people in leadership positions can emulate the behaviour that is proposed, will the others follow suit. Practice what you preach.

- *Handling Questions* – Do not neglect issues that worry your employees. A Change scenario can lead to a lot of questions regarding job security, workload, incentives etc. in the minds of those who are at the receiving end. And most of these are valid doubts. Therefore, in order to ensure long lasting support from your people, address these issues ASAP. Neglecting them will only compound and reaffirm their fears.

- *Two Way Communications* – A two way communication always permits a more candid exchange than a repressive one way communication. To the extent that it engages the employee and makes him feel valued, two way communications has a much more positive impact than merely dictating Changes.

ROLE OF TEAM LEADERS IN EACH BUSINESS DIVISION

Usually, an organisational Change initiative will involve more than one Business Unit. As a first step towards organising your Change efforts, identify all the units involved, directly or indirectly. For instance, your Change may directly involve a key functional area, but to accomplish the Change, you might need the help of other departments such as IT, Human Resource, Finance & Accounts and so on. Once you have identified the different business units involved, appoint a team leader for each unit, who will drive and lead the Change effort in that particular unit. Form a Steering Committee including the Change Agent, the Sponsors of Change, the CEO, and representatives from the different business units involved, to supervise the overall Change efforts.

Thus, the implementation of the plan is supervised at various levels – The Board of Directors supervises the CEO, the CEO supervises the Steering Committee, the Team Leaders in the Steering Committee serve as the link between the business units and the committee, and supervise the efforts of line employees. This structure ensures that the macro plan is implemented in a coordinated manner, and every unit is aware of their role and progress vis-à-vis the other units. However, at all levels, it is communication that binds the structure together. Hence, the line employees should regularly update the team leader of their progress, who in turn must share the same with the Steering Committee to ensure that Change happens in line with the broader objectives of the company.

```
THE BOARD OF DIRECTORS
          ↓
       THE CEO
          ↓
   STEERING COMMITTEE  →  Change Agent, Sponsor
                          Team representative, CEO
                       →  Team Leaders of the
                          different Business Units
                          ↓
                          Line Employees

NOTE: In addition to this framework, regular communication between the different levels is a must to ensure the success of change efforts.

KEY
⇒ = SUPERVISES
→ = COMPRISES
```

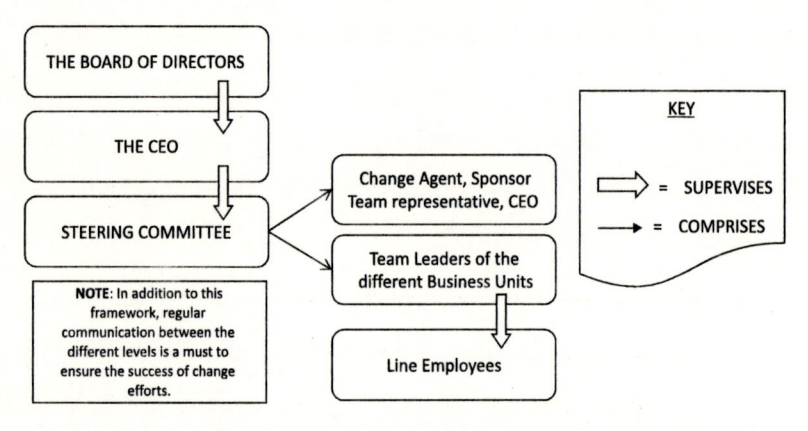

Figure 6.3 - A simple skeletal framework for effectively coordinating Change

Often, a Team Lead may have a large number of employees working under him. How does he go about ensuring that every individual is delivering the results expected on time? After all, he also has to tend to the daily management of routine activities in his area, besides driving Change efforts.

According to Weaver and Farell, "the most important role to emerge in the workplace" is that of a facilitator. In our context of organisational Change, facilitation is the primary responsibility of team leaders in all business divisions.

With the current emphasis on "downsizing" and reengineering to survive market situations, managers and team leads are faced with the problem of directing the work of a large number of people who report to them. It is important to realize that it is practically impossible to dictate the work of every individual. Rather, the tact lies in facilitating Change through delegation and learning rather than directing and spoon feeding. The manager can select a core group of individuals from among the large numbers that report to him. To this group, he provides guidelines of work, which are then translated into decisions by them. The decisions are then implemented by the mass of people in that team, through rapid learning and delegation of work. The core group can then perform the following set of activities:

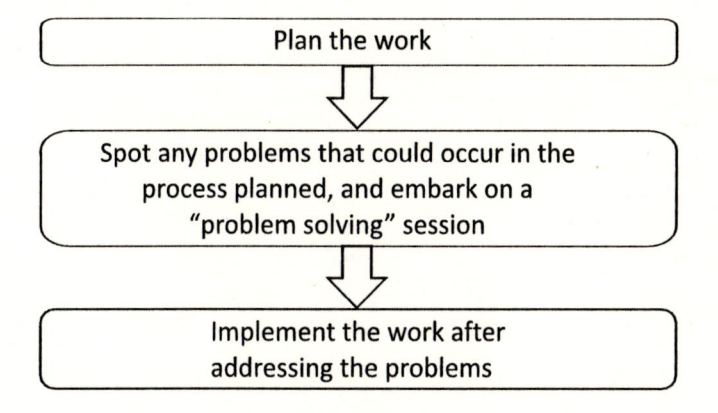

```
┌─────────────────────────────────────┐
│          Plan the work              │
└─────────────────────────────────────┘
                 ⇩
┌─────────────────────────────────────┐
│ Spot any problems that could occur  │
│ in the process planned, and embark  │
│    on a "problem solving" session   │
└─────────────────────────────────────┘
                 ⇩
┌─────────────────────────────────────┐
│   Implement the work after          │
│   addressing the problems           │
└─────────────────────────────────────┘
```

Figure 6.4 – Activities to be performed by Core Group

This is not only a better and more systematic way to handle work, it is also a good way to entrust your people with responsibility and empower them to take decisions. Often, in this process, employees themselves will become aware of their own capabilities of handling extreme situations independently.

Apart from managing Change efforts effectively, the team leaders also play an important role in emotionally supporting their team players. A Change situation throws up a lot of doubts and apprehensions. The team lead must appreciate that Change is difficult and be willing to address the concerns of his team members. Effective communication can offset Change related stress and anxiety, and thus positively impact productivity and efficiency. Face-to-face interactions, coaching or mentoring sessions may be organised to this effect.

Also, since the team lead works most closely with the employees, he can also judge their training needs and communicate the same to the Steering Committee, so that appropriate programs can be designed.

A very important responsibility of the team leader is to clarify to his team, what exactly is changing, the role of the team in bringing about the Change, and the responsibilities of individual team players in achieving the Change objective. The team lead could also set targets or define objectively measurable indicators that can measure the team's progress on a periodical basis.

The team lead should be one with exceptional field expertise, so that he can guide his team and provide it with information on available support and resources, in case it should get stuck.

Also, since he serves as the link between his team and the Steering Committee, he should ensure that consistent information from the Committee or the Board trickles down to them, and all decisions, activities and events are communicated on time.

COMMUNICATING ORGANISATIONAL CHANGE AT THE LOCAL LEVEL

Most often, organisational Change initiatives are conceived by the Board or top management but are executed at the local level. Hence, it is usually the team leaders who interact with the line employees in day-to-day implementation of Change plans.

The selection of the team leader therefore assumes paramount significance, as the credibility of the Change depends on the credibility of the one who communicates the Change. The more trusted the team leader is among his players, the more he can influence Change. However, trust stems from discovering the qualities of commitment, honesty, and empathy in the leader, and also hinges on his expertise, knowledge and experience. If the team leader can inspire trust and confidence among his mates, he can successfully drive the organisational Change initiatives.

It is important that in these interactions, there is a two way exchange between the team leaders and employees, so that area business processes can offer relevant feedback and suggestions to team leaders. This way, ground level concerns can be addressed and the necessary training and development provided.

This is absolutely essential, because once the Change has been accomplished; it is the area or line employees who will deal with the Changed circumstances on a daily basis. Hence, addressing their issues at the implementation stage helps avoid operational problems later. Thus, the Change is built on a strong foundation and tends to be long lasting.

Another benefit of a two way exchange is that it allows employees to openly voice their concerns, and hence induces a sense of control within them. This sense of security is important to them, for it is the lack of it in a Change scenario that leads to stress and resistance.

While communicating a Change at the local level, team leaders or managers need to understand that the more threatening the Change sounds, the more resistance it creates. Hence, managers must communicate Change in a manner that addresses perceived threats or risks and offsets them through potential benefits or incentives.

Effective communication of Change at the local level also involves articulating the benefits, which the proposed Change is expected to bring to the employees or their work area. This gives them a selfish real motive to support the Change and work towards it.

ESTABLISHING PERFORMANCE BENCHMARKS AND REWARDING PERFORMANCE

In order to measure the progress of Change efforts, set performance benchmarks and evaluate the performance of each team against these benchmarks. This will give you a feel of where you stand, and the gap that you need to close, to attain the desired Change. Share the findings with your employees, so they can act accordingly.

When team members know the deliverables, they can allocate resources and redefine processes to streamline their work. By sharing valuable feedback with them, you can help them fine tune their efforts to achieve results at a faster pace.

Tie your Change initiatives with performance assessment and incentives. Rewarding performance shows that individual Change efforts are respected and admired, and help to motivate similar efforts across the company.

FACE TO FACE PERFORMANCE REVIEWS

Face to face performance reviews help to address the personal concerns of your employees, and put their fears to rest. At the same time, it provides a platform where employees can openly discuss the challenges that they face in handling Change efforts along with routine activities. It thus provides an opportunity for you to clarify roles and expectations, mentor them and address their problems from their perspective. This, in turn, helps to maximize employee productivity and align personal goals with company objectives.

COMMUNICATION: A CONCLUDING NOTE

Communication is not simply the dissemination of information. The goal of communication is to Change the behavior of the audience, in a way that supports the organisational Change initiative, and only when this motive is accomplished can communication be termed as being "effective".

CHAPTER 7 /

Role of the CEO in Successful Organisational Change

One key to successful leadership is continuous personal change. Personal change is a reflection of our inner growth and empowerment.

~ Robert E. Quinn ~

Change is difficult to achieve because most often, it is faced with stiff opposition. While we have seen various reasons why employees resist change, opposition can come from top level people too. Studies have shown that change is often opposed by senior, elderly people because being a senior beginner comes across as unacceptable. People hate to think that processes and modes that they have executed all their life should suddenly seem redundant, rendering them useless unless they change themselves and adopt something new. Often, CEO's organize meetings to engage people in change activities, while themselves restricting their contribution to precious lip talk. As consistently emphasized throughout the text, the visible importance that the CEO attaches to change through his actions quickly becomes an index of how seriously employees perceive the change. To begin with, change is essentially a top-down activity. If the CEO perceives a certain change as indispensable and communicates the same to his people in practice, the entire organisation will follow suit. Once, the change is set in motion, it becomes an essentially down-up activity, where the ground level workforce implements the change plans, with top management and the CEO supervising and delegating work to them. Take a look at the figure below:

Role of the CEO in Successful Organisational Change

Phases of Change		A	B	C
Overall project Evaluation	PHASE 7			
Supervise the change at the unit level	PHASE 6			
Implement the Change	PHASE 5			
Drive the Change	PHASE 4			
Handle Resistance to Change	PHASE 3			
Communicate the need to change	PHASE 2			
Identify the need to change	PHASE 1			

Y Axis: Phases of Change
X Axis: Levels of Management
A: Lower Level Management & Line Employees
B: Middle Level Management
C: CEO and Top Level Management

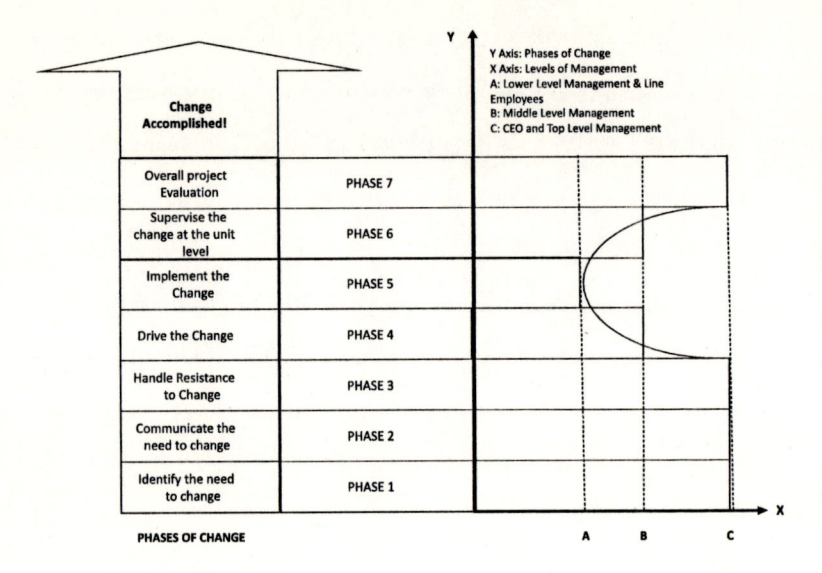

Figure 7.1 – Phases of Change

- The figure 7.1 shows a very simplistic analysis of the phases of change, and maps them against different levels of management that they are most closely associated with. Change is first conceived as an idea, a vision wherein the need for change is identified. It could either be a move towards a higher level of evolution or a move to correct a current aberration. The second phase involves communication of the need to change, and the third addresses the initial resistance to change. During all these phases, the CEO and top level management are the ones most closely involved. Once the initial resistance has been tackled, the focus shifts towards driving the Change and taking it forward (Phase 4 according to the diagram).

Here, a major role is played by the middle level management, although the importance of guidance and direction from the top level management cannot be undermined. The change is driven through appropriate change management plans, delegation of work and is finally implemented by the lower level managers and the line employees (Phase 5 in the diagram). Again, taking a rather simplistic view, we may say that these implementation efforts are followed by supervision by middle level managers (Phase 6). However, in practical situations, these two phases - 5 and 6 - may happen simultaneously rather than consecutively, probably involving middle level managers also in the implementation phase. The phases may thus evolve as a reiterative process of implementation, feedback from those impacted and supervision involving both lower and middle level of management. However, for the sake of convenience of representation, the figure shows them as two consecutive stages. Towards the end, the top level management comes into the picture again; as they evaluate the change progress against pre established indicators and goals of change. The graph thus roughly sketches a U-curve as the process moves from being top-down in the initial phases (till Phase 4) to bottom up (from Phase 5 onwards) in the later phases of change. Another thing to notice is the weight top management and the CEO carry in the whole process. Out of the 7 steps listed, CEO and top management are majorly involved in at least 4 phases. This clearly brings out the role of the CEO in organisational change.

Economics, I had read, is *"The science of optimum utilization of scarce resources."* These words probably best describe the scenario facing the CEO. At any given point in time, the company has a budget constraint - limited resources – in comparison to the areas which can be further developed or where changes can be profitably introduced. Thus, the CEO shoulders the primary responsibility of being able to choose from among the basket of changes, that one initiative which, if driven successfully, will help his company grow exponentially, and earn higher profits, faster than his competitors. Once the CEO takes this decision, the next step is to prepare a blueprint for success, an action plan that can place a foundation beneath his vision, that can transform his ideas into a concrete reality, and that can convince his people to get onboard!

Thus, organisation wide change is always a difficult proposition, and often the CEO must play a major role to ensure success. Broadly speaking, the CEO's role in Successful Organisational Change involves painting a vision, inspiring people to embrace the change, gathering political support, sustaining the energy and managing the transition phase.

```
                  ┌─────────────────┐                ┌─────────────────────┐
                  │ Managing the    │←──┐        ┌──→│ Painting a Powerful │
                  │ Transition Phase│──→│        │←──│ Vision              │
                  └─────────────────┘   │   ┌────┴┐  └─────────────────────┘
                                        └──→│ THE │
                                        ┌──→│ CEO │←──┐
                  ┌─────────────────┐   │   └────┬┘   │  ┌─────────────────┐
                  │ Sustaining the  │←──┘        │    └─→│ Inspiring People│
                  │ Energy          │──→         │    ←──│                 │
                  └─────────────────┘            ↓       └─────────────────┘
                                    ┌──────────────────────────┐
                                    │ Gathering Political support│
                                    └──────────────────────────┘
```

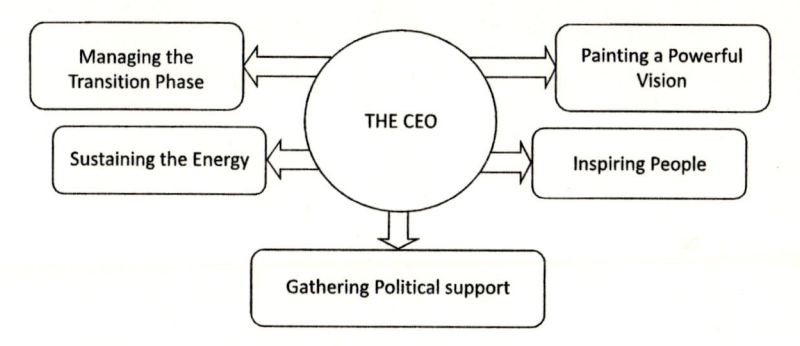

Figure 7.2 - CEO's role in successful organisational change

PAINTING A POWERFUL VISION

Creating an Effective Vision: What role does the CEO play?

— Communicate a powerful TRANSFORMATION STORY.

— Make the communication PERSONAL.

— Tie it with organisational CULTURE AND VALUES.

"What do you want to be when you grow up Karisma?" I asked. "Cinderella", my 5 year old replied, confidently.

Only when I looked up, a little startled, did I realize that she was watching the "Cinderella" show on TV. And then it occurred to me, that for any girl her age, it would be a dream come true, to move out of the daily drudgery of life (read:

HOMEWORK) into a beautiful, magical world of princes and palaces and ball dances and lovely clothes. Karisma wanted to "be" Cinderella, because her favorite show on air painted pictures for her that set her mind reeling.

Off late, Karisma wants to particularly use the pink Shampoo for her hair, because "it makes my hair thick and long". As you may have guessed, that is what the ad says.

In all forms of communication, which seek to impact behavior in one way or another, "painting a powerful picture" becomes the primary step. Communicating an organisational change is no different. A revolutionary concept will fail to inspire your people if you cannot make a powerful transformation story out of it. And here, the CEO has a major role to play. Given his position atop the hierarchy, the CEO inspires confidence and credibility. Hence, strong and meaningful vision, communicated by the CEO can maximize chances of success.

The power of the CEO's transformation story also depends on its ability to balance reality and dreams. A vision is born out of a dream, and many times it is a novel idea that drives the change. It is important to communicate to the people that there is nothing wrong in building castles in the air – you only need to place a strong foundation beneath them. The CEO needs to inspire a dream, and at the same time make it seem practically attainable.

Once, a certain agency delayed payment for my freelance services to them, by over 6 months. Repeated "gentle reminders", polite emails and numerous phone calls later, I finally decided it was time to barge in, and demand what I deserved. I don't know whether it was a coincidence, but within a week after I showed up at their office and said "The Press will welcome this news", my cheque came through.

The above situation may be incongruent to the discussion, but the lesson is important: Personal involvement elevates the significance of issues.

In the context of an organisational change, the CEO's personal involvement in communicating the change, either through his physical presence or vocally, can send across a very positive signal about the importance of change. This, in turn, motivates people to take up the challenge, participate in and support the change.

Finally, deep inside, employees identify best with organisational culture and values because these ideas form the basis of their informal organisation. Hence, tying the vision to organisational culture and values also form an important aspect of the CEO's communication.

INSPIRING CHANGE

The CEO's role in motivating the organisation

— Communicating the vision or the need for change

— Role Modelling Behaviour

— Personal Engagement in work floor issues

— Building a Strong Top Team

In order to inspire or motivate change, it is important to prepare people mentally for the change, and sustain their change efforts, besides communicating the need to change. The CEO plays a lead role here too. Let us see how.

Consider two situations. The first one: The CEO calls a meeting, makes an introductory communication regarding company values and mission, introduces a new vision, shares an action plan and directs all employees to participate in materializing the vision.

The second one: The CEO calls an informal meeting, celebrating the company's focused efforts in living up to its mission and core values, pushes the idea of a "new vision" or a "new organisation" amidst a lot of hearty jubilation, has bonnets, diaries or mugs carrying the mission, values and "new" vision on them distributed among people, takes their feedback on the proposed change and calls it a day. What a kick start to a new project!

Communicating a change is definitely not an easy task, but creating a positive vibe, building an atmosphere charged with enthusiasm right from the start and making people feel they are with you in this, rather than having them comply to your wishes, makes things a lot less tougher. And the CEO, as the leader of the organisation, is the best person to head this communication!

When I think of my schooldays, one prominent memory that keeps coming back to me is how big red circles and lines always adorned my papers, indicating the blunders that I had made.

Behavioral psychologists say that this method of evaluation, where the focus is always on the negatives can never promote learning in an organisation, especially in a change scenario.

Rather, to motivate change, it is important to emphasize on the positives and spotlight successful efforts. The CEO can play a meaningful role here. In the process of implementing change, the CEO could invite high performers to hold a presentation to the mass of people, showcasing their contribution. Sharing success stories gives confidence that the change will succeed. Further, giving value to such efforts in the form of rewards, incentives or promotions can fuel similar attempts across the organisation.

My 3 year old nephew doesn't understand why he needs to go to school. "Why can't I go to office like Daddy?" he asks. Apparently the logic that Daddy also had to go school, before he started working doesn't find much sense with him. "Well, I never saw him go to school, you know!" he frowns. Daddy, indeed, is his role model.

The CEO happens to be the "Daddy" of the organisation - the chief role model. And that is why, how he behaves or how he responds to a situation send out signals that the rest quickly pick up. In a change scenario, this means that the CEO needs to role model the expected behavior. Always under the spotlight, the CEO is literally required to be the change he wishes to see. For, in the last instance, people study his actions to decide whether his story is credible or not. His behavior becomes the index of his own passion and drive and thus, if the CEO's personal conduct reflects the change he summons, employees will follow suit. However, this may require a conscious effort on the part of the CEO. In order to ensure that he sends out appropriate signals to the organisation, he might need to set himself a target list of personal commitments in line with the change objectives, or alternatively keep a tab on the amount of quality time that he spends on change initiatives etc. It helps when executives in several leadership positions undertake similar activities along with the CEO, reinforcing and supporting each other's personal transformation odyssey.

A CEO who prefers a visit to the plant is more capable of inspiring his team than one who stays behind in his executive suite. The CEO's personal engagement in resolving operational bottlenecks serves as an indicator of how important the project is, and acts as a major motivating force.

Team building is important. Just as a car can run only on four wheels, change initiatives can work only though organized team efforts. In this direction, the CEO can contribute towards establishing a top team of influential and effective leaders, who can coordinate the work of different teams and guide change through difficult times.

GATHERING POLITICAL SUPPORT

Power Play, Change and the CEO

— Secure the support of the Board, Senior Management and key power players

— Involve power players at all key stages in the process

— Appreciate, evaluate and act upon their suggestions or recommendations

In the context of an organisation, power can denote several attributes. Power comes from knowledge, experience and expertise; it also comes from personal qualities such as an ethical, upright personality, honesty and integrity. Power is derived from the authority that one commands and is often tied to one's hierarchical position in the organisation chart.

In a scenario of change, it is important to realize that the organisation needs specific resources and skills to carry out its objectives. And most often, it is the ones in power who exercise authority over these resources. For instance, you need a certain number of people to man your change efforts, but some of them work in a different department. The Chief of that Department however will not release them for your activities, since these are key people already involved in some other task that is urgent and important. Your initiative demands a budget that the Finance & Accounts department doesn't second. The HR Department feels you are creating too many vacancies by diverting too many people from their current responsibilities and moving them to permanent task forces to support your project. At every stage, people in power wield authority over resources that you will need for your project. And therefore to ensure the success of your project, you must ensure the support of all key power players like the Board, Senior Management etc. The CEO, while himself being a major power player, can help in securing the support of key power positions to ensure smooth running of the project.

It is also important to ensure that all key power players have a say in the vision, policy making and communication of change and any concerns or recommendations voiced by them must be immediately acted upon.

MANAGING TRANSITION

Once a change process sets in, the transition from the old to a new set of circumstances stands out as the toughest challenge.

Appropriate coaching and training help build the required skills, but periodical mentoring or motivational sessions are also required to boost the energy of the team. Enforcement of new policies corresponding to the change objectives and sustained communication on the need to change and status of change are also important. Further, managing transition also includes taking stock of the gap between perceived and achieved goals. As stressed earlier, periodical evaluation of projects, face to face meetings with team leaders or team members, inviting responses from team members, etc. play an important role in this direction.

All these activities are best implemented when integrated into a well drawn out Change Management Plan, with pre defined deadlines. Although, unpredictable contingencies may deter strict adherence to such plans, regular evaluation against pre established performance indicators, and sharing the results of the evaluation with team members can ensure that progress is "on track". Project evaluation against a pre-established "team charter", also help to ensure that progress is aligned to the larger objectives of change. A team charter is an agreement of all team members on what they want to achieve and how they want to achieve. It also contains an understanding of the expected and acceptable behaviour within the team.

With this objective, the CEO can organise Review meetings to understand the gap between the original plan and the current status, detect the root cause of operational issues and explore strategies to resolve them. Also, it is important that, as a part of these meetings, the CEO assigns team leaders with the responsibility of aligning change activities with change objectives, and showing visible results as per the pre established indicators. This ensures that the teams never lose sight of the macro objectives, even as they grapple with daily operational issues and other roadblocks.

The key role of the CEO during such review meetings is to ensure that all decision making is anchored only in facts, and that there is a healthy balance between attainment of short term goals and long term objectives in the process of driving change.

SUSTAINING THE ENERGY

Change initiatives are seldom free from barriers. Various factors such as strong resistance to change, sudden resignation of key people or shift of focus on other exigencies that need immediate attention, may impede the momentum of change efforts. Therefore, a major responsibility of the CEO and Top Management is to sustain the energy of team members, and steer the process through difficult times. This involves lending mental support and motivation to the employees, when work gets stuck, ensuring that proper knowledge base and technical skills are available at every stage of implementation, identifying training needs and developing appropriate programs, planning work in a manner that responds to both short term and long term goals of the organisation etc. Support from the CEO during the transition phase revitalizes change efforts, and reinforces the significance of the project to the company's overall vision. For instance, the CEO taking a fifteen minute walk around the plant every day can do wonders at pulling out people from bouts of low morale or dipping spirits, which are not uncommon during transition. It is a symbolic act signifying that your people are valued for their contribution, and this helps sustain the energy at work. The CEO and top management should explore all available options and organize meetings, video conferences, video meetings, in-house newspapers and other publications to reach out to the people. Appreciation can work wonders. At the end of the day, the CEO must realize that transition is difficult, and while results may be visible only in time, employees are perhaps going through their toughest phase. CEO's who can withstand the pressures of a delayed reflection of change initiatives in financial reports and instead appreciate individual efforts during this phase can miraculously step up energy levels. Employee Performance Management Systems can be used as a tool in this stage, to periodically interact with employees, hold face to face meetings wherein, goals and roles can be clarified and private concerns can be addressed and discussed. This helps the top management to connect holistically with those on the work floor, build relationships and help the employees stay in sync with the larger objectives of change.

Some Basic Competencies of the CEO required to successfully handle Change

Heading the organisation is not an easy task, especially when it is undergoing a transition. Some of the basic skills and competencies that CEO's must display, to successfully steer the organisation through change include the following:

1. **Goal Setting and Leadership Skills:** This refers to the ability to proactively judge present developmental needs and strategically decide upon an appropriate change initiative. This calls upon the CEO's ability to analyze the present situation, foresee the future, anticipate challenges and take quick and correct decisions. At the same time, leadership skills enable the CEO to ensure that his people

buy the change and follow him energetically in making it happen.

2. **Planning Skills:** Good planning skills are required to enable the attainment of goals. While detailed planning takes place at a later stage, the CEO needs to have in mind at least a skeletal plan, which makes the change seem convincing and helps him sell it to his people.

3. **Problem Solving Skills:** One of the most important skills a CEO needs to have is the ability to solve problems in a simple and quick manner. A change process is seldom without problems. As and when the change progresses, new problems are encountered and these must be timely settled to effectively steer change.

4. **Integrity and Charisma:** This is more relevant than we normally think. The CEO's personality impacts, in a big way, how people perceive him or react to his ideas. A dynamic, magnetic personality is more capable of influencing others to follow direction than a passive and unapproachable one.

5. **Communication Skills:** Coaching, counseling and

mentoring are required at various stages of the change program. This requires the CEO to be firm yet sensitive to people concerns and address them in a way that inspires security and confidence. Nurturing trust, handling difficult people, motivating others, providing an honest feedback etc. all fall under the purview of effective communication that forms the link between the CEO and his people. The stronger the link, the stronger is the relationship between the organisation and its people, and the stronger is their commitment and loyalty to the company.

6. **Team Building Skills and Directing Work:** The CEO must have a clear picture of how the humongous task of change can be best carried out through delegation of activities.

7. **Supervising and Evaluating Skills:** The CEO must be able to evaluate progress along the correct dimensions. Supervision at his level involves not only overseeing whether the work progresses as per plan but also anticipating challenges and devising next steps in advance.

Concluding Note

Uncertainty, risk and change are the three inevitable forces that drive all businesses across the globe. Uncertainty is beyond control. Risk can also be anticipated or calculated only to some extent. Change, on the other hand, can be initiated and planned.

In order to stay competitive in a business environment, that is continuously evolving and upgrading itself, CEO's need to proactively steer their companies through a maze of changes, with the impact spanning over a unit or the entire organisation. In very large companies, different strategic business units may have different goals, customer sets and strategies etc. In these cases, the head of the business unit may dispense the role of the CEO, for practical considerations. Whatever the case, throughout the change process, the CEO must continue to lead and support all that goes on at the lower levels to help materialize the change.

They say "With great power comes great responsibility", and the CEO's role in change is but a visible manifestation of this. Many best practice organisations feel that the CEO's involvement is a must to ensure success, and with the power, foresight, knowledge and experience that the CEO of an organisation commands, there is hardly room for a second opinion!

CHAPTER 8 /

Attributes of CEO and Organisational Change

People can't live with change if there's not a changeless core inside them. The key to the ability to change is a changeless sense of who you are, what you are about and what you value.

~ Stephen Covey ~

Another success.

Another celebration...

Marcus looked around him. Chris, as usual, was gorging away, that smiling rubicund had been his strongest support all these years. Much had changed, I-Systems had come a long way since they'd completed that first project, and Marcus reveled in the thought that they had already been around for 15 years now!

Talking of change....ah well! The company had performed spectacularly well. A major merger with an industry giant had followed. They had grown by multiples and had successfully completed projects in China, Indonesia and Thailand. Today, with employee strength of about 200 people, I-Systems could boast of a strong customer base that spanned across various countries in the Asia-Pacific...And there was more. Kay had left the organisation. Significant business needs had demanded Marcus's attention as the CMO of I-Systems. Steve Martin had taken over as the CEO.

Yes! A lot had changed, and changed for the better. Yet, 15 years down the line, sitting here today, celebrating another success, Marcus was gravely disturbed. Something was wrong, and he could sense it. Instinctively, he knew, and in fact he could clearly see, that they were moving, yet without a sense of direction. Something was amiss. Steve had steered some strategic changes in his initial years, but in the last few years, Marcus had sensed in him certain complacency. That Steve did not carry industry experience also went against him sometimes, Marcus thought, though that had seemed quite an advantage initially.

Today, after so many years as CEO, CTO and now CMO of I-Systems, Marcus wondered whether things would be better if he took charge!

....

What went wrong with Steve? Why was it that he performed so well in his initial years but lost tempo later? Or how did his not having industry experience impact performance? In recent times, a lot of weight has been given to studying the attributes of CEOs in relation to firm performance. It has been widely concluded that several "CEO attribute" parameters considerably influence the CEO's attitude towards change, and hence impact the firm's strategic decisions and performance. Various factors such as CEO experiential attributes, tenure, personal development vis-à-vis firm evolution, functional background, functional diversity, gender and origin exercise a sizeable influence on CEO attitude to change and hence companywide performance. Recent surveys, in general, have indicated that CEO tenure is inversely relational to strategic organisational changes, while the effect of other factors on the CEO's attitude towards change are seen to diminish in impact with the increase in tenure. This chapter explores five CEO attributes – tenure, experiential attributes, origin, functional background and personal development through research results of various surveys conducted till date, and aims to provide the reader, wherever possible, an insight into some aspects of characteristic behavior which can be consciously managed to yield higher firm performance.

CEO TENURE AND ATTITUDE TOWARDS CHANGE

Research across several companies at several points in time has consistently indicated that top executive tenure and organisational change are inversely related to each other.

Gabarro (1987), Finkelstein and Hambrick (1990), Grimm and Smith (1991) and then Wiersema and Bantel (1992) all concluded from their surveys that the tenure of top executives in a company shares a negative relationship with change in the company.

Thus, it is possible to discern from their findings that in

general, CEOs tend to introduce substantial changes during the initial phases of their tenure. However, towards the later phases this tendency shows a decline, as they become conservative to change.

One reason why top executives seem to respond to change vis-à-vis tenure in this manner could be that when they are new to the company, they see it as an entity that can be molded in any desirable fashion. However, with time, this vision becomes more constrained by the history and current status quo of the company, adversely impacting their openness to change.

Another finding suggests a probable reason for the abovementioned behavior as stemming from the willingness to take risks. It was found that executives with a shorter tenure are more maverick, open to taking risks and experimenting with non conformist strategies. They are more open to taking chances and reaching out for new opportunities. Conversely, with the increase in tenure, executives displayed lower risk taking capacities, rather preferring to follow established strategies and conforming to the mainstream trend.

Tenure and Change

In the later phases of their tenure, there is a shift in executives from exploration to exploitation wherein they start reaping the benefits of all that they have learned during the initial phases of their tenure. So, all the knowledge that was acquired through experience and experimentation during the earlier half goes into a reserve, from where it is pulled out at will, to address similar situations later.

This is an area that demands attention and is a bit disconcerting because this complacency that builds up, leads to non exploration of creative and innovative solutions to problems, leading to imitative, reiterative approaches that may have actually become obsolete in the current environment. It is an instance of Simmerman's Square Wheels Metaphor in practice, where better solutions exist, but are never explored, because things seem to be moving forward, anyway! For instance, just because the current product is doing well in the market, executives may not explore market trends, which may show considerable opportunities for other products in a similar line. Hence, the company may actually forgo a grand opportunity of stepping up market share, and expand business. Thus, the executive complacency that comes with an increase in tenure can lead to precious loss, if not consciously addressed. Especially, in the rapidly changing global environment that exists today, lack of dynamism can spell danger, and could turn the relationship between executive tenure and company performance increasingly negative.

Interestingly, as an extension to these findings, a subsequent survey found that not only company tenure, but even industrial tenure bears an inverse relationship with strategic organisational change. In fact, industrial tenure was found to impact attitude to change to a much greater extent than did company tenure. So, the greater the executive tenure in the company, organisation or industry, the more is the resistance to strategic change. This needs deliberate attention as undue resistance could stagnate business by not exploring strategic business opportunities.

CEO EXPERIENTIAL ATTRIBUTES AND ORGANISATIONAL CHANGE

Knowledge and experience are two invaluable assets that empower the CEO to consistently add value to his organisation. Knowledge comprises not only conscious learning that CEOs accumulate through experience, but also tacit knowledge that work-related practical know-how brings. Thus, apart from knowledge that is amassed consciously, there is also a lot of knowledge picked up informally or unconsciously. This infinite stockpile of tacit knowledge inventory (TKI) comprises the basis of what is commonly known as intuition. How much of tacit knowledge a CEO picks up from his experience, however, is subjective and varies with his individual propensity to glean out learning's from different situations.

Tacit knowledge influences a lot of decisions taken by top executives. While, as rational beings, we tend to prefer structured decisions, guided by strong reason, not all decisions at the top are based on formal analysis. This is when intuition is being applied to judge situations. In strategic decision making, there needs to be a proper balance of both rationale and intuition.

What makes intuitive knowledge relevant to strategic change situations, which require quick decision making, is that intuitive decisions are often faster taken than rational ones. Eisenhardt (1989, 1990) and Bourgeois and Eisenhardt (1988) studied the speed of strategic decisions by CEOs in the California computer industry, and concluded that the increased speed of decisions could be attributed significantly to the use of intuition!

Further, Wagner and Sternberg (1987) found that TKI differed in relation to people's experience. Moreover if this experience is marked by consistent professional attainment, the level of tacit knowledge increases accordingly. In fact, a higher level of tacit knowledge itself is associated with higher performance ratings. Considering the height of professional elevation, experience and knowledge that the CEO has scaled, it is possible to discern that they also command a high level of tacit or intuitive knowledge.

Wagner (1991) concluded from his research that the use of the rational thought and level of tacit knowledge complement each other during strategic business. While early literature on strategic management laid greater emphasis on the application of rationality and formal analysis in decision making, recent research shows that with growing uncertainty and an ever changing external environment, a more informal process based on trial and experience is required to face change. CEOs who can successfully apply intuition are better equipped to take quick strategic decisions, and hence derive advantage from short-lived opportunities in a dynamic environment, thus increasing the chances of better firm performance.

Ansoff (1988) contends that strategic knowledge can

particularly be gained only tacitly or experientially. So, with experience and exposure to diverse problems and their solutions, the mind builds up an immense stock of problems and their related solutions. A similar situation encountered in future then activates a recall function, which draws upon this previous experience to generate an intuition about the situation. Thus, on the premise that increased experience leads to an increased level of TKI, it is possible to discern that the experienced CEO's use of TKI can temper his response to change and escalate firm performance.

A later research however, has thrown up two more perspectives to this. Not always does an experienced CEO aptly utilize his intuitive power. In fact, application of tacit knowledge was found to be tied to:

Individual Propensity – The individual CEO's capacity to draw upon the TKI and evaluate situations.

Industry Experience – More than current organisational experience or generic experience (that can also be considered a function of CEO age), industry experience was found to have a more profound impact on the use of tacit knowledge in strategic decision making. This could be because industrial experience across different organisations in the same industry leads to a better understanding of industry dynamics. This, in turn, helps to draw a better analysis of the competitive environment, which significantly impacts organisational change decisions.

The Learning

What CEOs consciously need to monitor is a balanced use of experiential or tacit knowledge. Non application of this knowledge inventory can lead to inability to take quick decisions and gain strategic advantage, whereas excessive reliance on tacit knowledge, disregarding current market trends can lead to a "I know the answer" kind of a situation, where they might give in to complacency and resort to conveniently drawing out solutions from a reserve, rather than creatively exploring better solutions.

CEO ORIGIN, STRATEGIC CHANGE AND FIRM PERFORMANCE

Strategic Change refers to a variation in the firm's resource allocation in key strategic dimensions, to respond to a changing environment or to establish a strategic advantage over competitors. In some cases, this change may be triggered by a change in the industry's competitive environment, wherein all firms in the industry adopt a similar kind of resource allocation change. In these situations, an individual firm's change decision will more or less mirror the industry-wide deviation.

A firm's strategic change in this sense can work in two ways. It can either help the company align itself to the industry environment, in which case it is an adaptive change improving firm performance, or it can lead to non alignment and/or poor performance due to inefficient implementation, in which case it is a disruptive change. Decades of research have gone into addressing the question of how CEO origin affects organisational outcomes. Because insider CEOs and outsider CEOs both come with distinctly different portfolios in terms of knowledge and experience, they have distinctly different impacts on the firm's performance. Insider CEOs come with more firm-specific knowledge such as company history, past performance, specific strengths and weaknesses etc., whereas Outsider CEOs may be better equipped with non-firm specific but relatively new or different skill sets derived from industry experience, which can be instrumental in shaping the organisation. Hence, the origin of the CEO influences his take on strategic change decisions and hence impacts firm performance.

Subsequently conducted survey results have concluded that the level of strategic change has an inverted U-shaped relationship with firm performance.

Thus, while change varies between slight and moderate, firm performance improves but as the intensity of change increases from moderate to great, firm performance declines. More interestingly, this inverted U-shaped relationship differs between firms led by outside CEOs and those led by inside CEOs. Thus, results show that both the positive impact of strategic change on firm performance (at a relatively lower level of change) and the negative impact of strategic change on firm performance (at a relatively higher level of change)

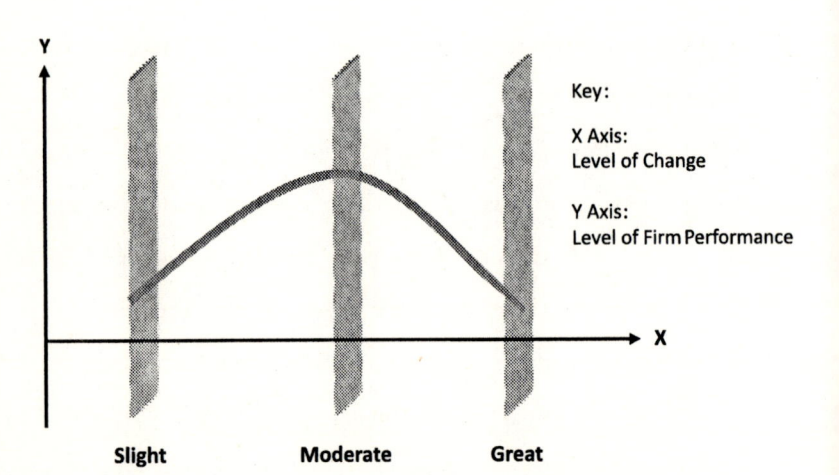

Figure 8.1 – U-shaped relationship of strategic change with firm performance

are amplified for outside CEOs than for inside CEOs.

It is argued that, relative to inside CEOs; outside CEOs magnify both the adaptive and the disruptive effects of strategic change. There are various reasons to support this. Outside CEOs can multiply the adaptive effect because often times, they are hired to control an imminent danger, due to a decline in performance, which means changes that they initiate to address the situation already have the support of key external and internal agents. Also, the fact that they are new to the organisation means they are free of any biases tied to the status quo. Additionally, when they come from a different organisation in the same industry, they bring with them a different perspective, or different skill sets, which may enable them to successfully lead strategic change initiatives.

However, in comparison to inside CEOs, outside CEOs have only limited knowledge when it comes to firm specific information, for instance its strengths, weaknesses, resources etc. Hence, they may not be able to identify a company's strategic vantage points and select an appropriate type or level of change, suitable for the organisation, at that given point in time. Not being able to identify vantage points could be a disadvantage from the change perspective, because it is easier to capitalize on existing competencies rather than summon entirely new ones, especially if immediate results are required. At higher levels of strategic change, this is combined with the risk of failure and higher implementation costs, which can further amplify the disruptive effect.

Supplementary analyses also indicate that this difference between outside and inside CEOs in the relationship between levels of strategic change and firm performance exists more distinctly in the later years than in the early years of CEO tenure. Researchers say that a possible explanation is that outside CEOs are, as we saw earlier, mostly hired to handle immediate changes, and so their efforts are more often directed towards cost cutting and divestment in the early years of their tenure. As tenure increases, the obvious opportunities for cost cutting and divestment are all eventually exploited and the focus shifts to long term growth. Thus, the advantage of a different skill set or perspective that the outsider CEO brings to the company is utilized during the early half to initiate strategic changes, but eventually dry up and lose sheen. These findings provide guidelines that are useful when deciding upon a successor CEO in the face of an ever changing business environment, so as to appropriately address business needs.

CEO FUNCTIONAL BACKGROUND & DIVERSITY AND ORGANISATIONAL CHANGE

Functional backgrounds of CEOs imply their job experience within the organisation or within the industry.

In general, a lengthy association with a single company endows the CEO with more company specific knowledge; whereas a diverse association with several companies in the same industry can offer valuable and different insights into the industry dynamics. Past industry experience of CEOs help them to form mental impressions of events and situations, which then function like cognitive maps, to guide them in better analyzing or interpreting the competitive environment, and to take wiser and more holistic strategic decisions in similar situations later. Thus, firm strategies of companies whose CEOs have had a strong functional background, spanning different companies, are often better tailored to achieve a competitive edge in the industry.

In fact, the CEO's industry experience not only carries performance implications for his organisation, but also has an important bearing on the organisations' tendency to undertake strategic change. Statistical research suggests that strategic change is negatively correlated with longer single industry experience (Wiersema & Bantel, 1992) and top managers with lower average industry experience with one firm have been found to be more open to adopting changes rather than implementing set work patterns (Bantel, 1993). This is because the longer one serves a single organisation, the more they conform to the existing culture, and the higher is the commitment to the status quo. This, in turn, adversely affects the firm's propensity to change strategically (Hambrick, et al., 1993).

Again, the perspectives of CEOs with single industry experience will differ from those of CEOs who have experienced diverse industries. In our ever changing business environment, a change in the external environment throws up a new set of operating conditions for firms, and demand that they align their processes accordingly. Therefore, in order to be able to respond to such changes appropriately, it is imperative to be able to perceive those changes, in their entirety. Fresh perspectives deriving from the CEO's past inter industry experience offer a prismatic view of the situation at hand, and hence affect strategic change decisions that can lead to better firm performance. Previous research suggests that the perceptions of CEOs tempered by broader industry experience, through service to multiple industries, widened their spectrum of strategic choices and improved firm performance. Thus, firms with low levels of performance often seek CEOs with a different background and perspective from outside the industry.

As and when a company evolves, it passes through various phases or life cycle stages. Every phase demands a higher and more complex understanding of the business environment and strategic vantage points to be able to navigate to the next level of evolution. Porter (1985) contends that it would be rare to find one CEO who possesses the necessary background and experience, to be able to steer the organisation through all of its various life cycle stages. Thus, as firms pass through these stages, strategic changes prompt many firms to change their CEOs. Depending on business needs, industry experience of the new CEO then becomes a major selection criterion.

Also, when their "generic" work experience is more diverse, CEOs often develop a greater ability to deal with different environmental factors, and become more empowered to envision complex situations, such as diverse businesses. This has a positive impact on the organisation's ability to conceptualize and capitalize on strategic change opportunities and hence magnify firm performance. Further, CEOs with more extensive executive level management have been found to display higher levels of performance, evidenced by better asset management and hence firm performance.

CEO EGO DEVELOPMENT STAGES AND ORGANISATIONAL CHANGE

Yet another year.

Call it coincidence, fate or luck.

As Marcus readied himself for the Board meet, he felt an eerie sense of déjà vu. Steve had resigned last month, citing personal reasons, and today's Board meet would officially declare him the Group CEO of I-Systems.

Steve's resignation had taken him by surprise, and at first, he had felt abandoned. At a time, when the company was losing direction and needed focused, strong leadership, his CEO was quitting the show!! For some time now, Marcus had even deliberately pushed back a small part of him, which kept saying - perhaps it was time he took charge. But with the Board proposing the same, Marcus had had to give it a serious thought and so today, was the D - Day.

Over the next few weeks, Marcus took stock of the situation, planning rigorous sessions with Steve and charting how he might bring a transformation.

A month passed, and Steve departed. Marcus finally took over the role he had been officiating in the past one month. That day, at the gathering which was organized to formally introduce him to his employees as the new Group CEO, Marcus made a "kick-start". After a brief informal talk on his personal journey, wherein he shared bits and pieces of his struggles and successes, with his people, Marcus announced a new vision statement! Amidst loud cheers and applause Marcus ended the day with a promise to himself – Within the next 2 years, he would have his people live the vision.

In the following few months, he identified key people who would help him drive the organisation. He got some experienced people onboard and used one of these new senior guys to pen down his vision statement into a strategic plan. He had realized that as a global organisation now, it would be a good idea to tap the Indian market and that meant a new operational setup and of course more change!! Several rounds of weekly meetings with the board and parent company followed, convincing them about his plans and the kinds of investment it would warrant. They would have to set up new departments, new activities, and choose new people to lead those.

Next, once a week he started communicating with the ground level employees, and fresh entrants, educating them and sharing with them their vision. He met all the important customers, who were facing critical problems and personally worked upon them to see that technical, commercial, legal issues were addressed.

And at the rate, at which they were progressing, he knew he would not disappoint himself. Yes! He knew he had a promise to live up to....

In a particularly interesting revelation, a research by David Rooke and William R. Torbert identified some startling analogies between the personal development stages of the CEO and the Organisational Development stages, concluding that the personal development stage of the CEO has a direct impact on attitude to organisational change.

As I emphasized in the past few chapters, collective responsibility and collaborative efforts are absolutely essential to steer successful change initiatives. To carry people along, educate them about the company's vision and secure their support for the change initiative is an imperative for change success. Something that Marcus did, isn't it?

Rooke and Torbert's research shows that leaders, who realize that mutual and voluntary efforts, rather than hierarchical guidance, are required to affect a successful change initiative, are more likely to succeed in leading organisational transformation.

No kind of power exercised unilaterally can result in enduring change. Rather, it is only when CEOs appreciate the difficulty of change and acknowledge themselves as being as vulnerable to the change as their employees can a sustainable change effort be driven.

This realization, however, was seen to come at a relatively later stage in the cognitive-emotional development of most CEOs, signified in their research by late-stage leaders at the Strategist stage or beyond. To know more about the analogies between the personal and organisational stages of development, look at the table below.

According to developmental theory and workplace research (Fisher & Torbert, 1995), the first stage at which a leader can begin organisational development in a manner that is mutually conducive to genuine personal and organisational learning, rather than through the use of power or coercion, is the Strategist/Leader stage (Stage 6 in the table). This stage however occurs near the end of the personal developmental stage model, as given in the table.

ANALOGIES BETWEEN PERSONAL AND ORGANISATIONAL DEVELOPMENT STAGES

Stage	Personal Development	Organisational Development
1	You are ruled by Impetuous behavior as multiple impulses demand your attention.	A new Organisation vision is conceived and attempts are made to align multiple impulses and resolve them into a planned approach.
2	You move from being plain impulsive to tutoring your behavior towards attaining the end in view. Often, you behave like an opportunist, seeking to make the best of what you have so as to be able to achieve your goal. This phase can see you turning manipulative, even deceptive when you decide to attain your end within a restrained time frame in mind. You flout rules, become a maverick, disregard constructive feedback and want to have it your way.	Financial investments are made, social networks, peer networks are built and commitment is sought from champions to create the envisioned organisation etc.

3	At the next stage, you realize that to be able to achieve your goal, you need the help of others. You stick to protocol, conform to norms, and are nice and cooperative, endeavoring to "fit in".	At this stage, called the incorporation stage, the organisation has a goal, a physical setup and some employees. Roles and responsibilities are assigned to them so as to actually start turning out goods or services. Organisation starts adapting to respond to a wider market and consistent attempts are made to bridge the gap between the envisioned and the actual organisation.
4	You display expertise and positive ethics. You are a perfectionist and as critical of others as of your own self. You indulge in rigorous problem solving, root cause search and give a lot of emphasis on efficiency. Stage marked by intellectual mastery.	Creativity, innovation and experimentation with alternative strategies, testing and reforming them, with the objective of finding a lasting combination of strategy and structure. Stage marked by innovation to discover what works best.
5	You become result oriented and strive to meet your own standards. You view the future as a world of possibilities and opportunities and	Focus shifts to systematic procedures, productivity for attaining predefined objectives; viability of the

	set long term objectives. You appreciate constructive feedback and engage yourself in practical day-to-day improvements, adhering to a certain ethical system.	product or service, marketability as being quantitatively measurable, assumes significance, standards and structures are taken as already formalized and reality is perceived in terms of dichotomies, black and white, good and bad, personal and professional etc.
6	Strategist/Leader stage when you creatively involve yourself in resolution of conflicts, maintain good decisions, respect individuality, diversity and difference in opinion, become both process oriented and goal oriented.	Explicit collaborative efforts, sharing the corporate mission and vision, open conversation or feedback with and from individual employees, Stronger interpersonal relationships emerge, differences are valued and systematic evaluation of corporate and individual performance against multiple parameters takes place; Commitment to a unique self-amending structure for the organisation, that endorses what is best for the organisation at that given point in time.

7	You pass into a phase where you seek spiritual transformation, erase dichotomies, become introspective and intuitive and treat time and events as being symbolic of a higher meaning.	Explore the shared research on the connections between the spiritual, theoretical and behavioral aspects of experience, structure fails but shared goals and purpose drive the organisation.
8	You become an ironist.	Leadership practices a precarious liberation, introduces a deliberate irony of assigning tasks that are incomprehensible, the organisational structure remains open, and in principle, members can scrutinize and challenge leadership if tasks, processes, and mission become incongruous and leadership does not acknowledge and appropriately address such incongruities.

CHAPTER 9 /

Role of the CEO in Succession Planning

Never doubt that a small, group of thoughtful, committed citizens can change the world. Indeed, it is the only thing that ever has.

~ Margaret Mead ~

Things were looking up once again. Marcus's plans of starting a new setup in India had taken off well and this was their third year in operation. A booming market, the Indian venture had brought them phenomenal growth, and had been the singular turning point since Steve left.

Marcus closed his eyes and thought back. Of the days when he had started the company as a young man, of how he had brought in Kay, then bid him adieu, of how he had brought in Steve who had bid him adieu, of how he had worried that his company was on the rocks, and of how, like a Phoenix, it had risen from its own ashes, spreading its wings over a trebled empire.

He smiled.

He had lived up to his promise, and his people had lived up to their vision. But there was something more.

Steve's departure had come as a rude shock to him.... But, like every mishap, it had also brought an important learning. And now, something told him that perhaps it was time to put his learning to practice...Yes, if he wanted his company to grow, he would have to put the company's progress above his own....

Sound planning essentially precedes effective crisis management. This common knowledge when applied to the area of organisational leadership triggers what is known as Succession Planning. This chapter discusses succession planning, elaborating on the role of the CEO in the process.

WHAT IS SPM?

"Succession Planning and Management, or SPM, refers to the planned, systematic efforts undertaken by an organisation with the objective of ensuring leadership continuity. It includes:

- Identifying key positions in the organisation
- Assigning a set of essential competencies to these roles
- Identifying potential holders for these roles; and
- Developing them to take on these roles

It can be considered as an investment in intellectual capital that serves as a buffer for leadership crisis.

However, far from being a help tool when crisis actually strikes, succession planning should be undertaken as part of the talent management and people development functions

– a continuous, ongoing process. This was the learning that Steve's departure had brought for *Marcus*.

WHY IS SUCCESSION PLANNING ESSENTIAL?

According to Wayne Bleakley, succession planning should focus on senior management positions, starting at the head of the organisation chart (with special emphasis on the CEO and/or managing director) and going down to include the middle management. Some others argue that Succession Planning should happen throughout the entire organisation and at all levels.

But why is succession planning so important? According to Levensaler (Bersin & Associates, 2008), the present volatile business environment throws up Nine key challenges for organisations. Leading among them are:

1. Leadership gaps and performance, and

2. Filling key roles and retaining talent.

(This information is based on data gathered from the USA, Asia Pacific, Europe & the Middle East (EMEA)).

Further, the NYSE Listed Company Manual indicates that CEO succession planning is one of the seven primary tasks of the board of directors. But the intricacies involved in the process have often left the Board in a lurch.

Various factors such as accidents, sudden demise, retirement, resignation etc. may lead to the loss of a leader in the organisation. Strong succession planning helps to address this leadership crisis and to sustain healthy investor relationships even through turbulent times.

Also, given the unending changes that characterize the business environment today, the CEO's role has become increasingly challenging and dynamic. In such a scenario, many times, it is CEO underperformance that leads to leadership crisis.

When Yahoo!'s Terry Semel joined the company in 2001, and subsequently drove it to towering heights, no one would have thought that six years later, this same man would need to step down. The reason? Changes in the business environment, the entry of a sturdy competitor – Google, and the implications on his role as CEO. The board soon discovered that with the focus now shifting to discovery of new markets and diversification into new businesses, Semel's role demanded entirely different skill sets, and soon in 2007, thought it better to replace him. An otherwise successful CEO, Semel, fell prey to a changing external market environment.

Further, globalization has opened the doors to a whole lot of collaborations, mergers and acquisitions. These, in turn are accompanied by the need to adapt to changes in culture, a change in focus and more competition. Clearly, underperformance is the one thing that stands no chance. In fact, it has been seen that immediately after an acquisition private equity firms characteristically replace their presiding CEOs, with a new CEO who they believe possesses the required skill set to steer the organisation.

Succession Planning helps to prepare companies to meet such crises. Hence, if not effectively carried out, it can set off an ugly recoil effect with political power plays clouding the replacement process, monetary losses or loss of direction due to disabled leadership and loss of critical knowledge. This, in turn, can adversely impact work and employee morale.

The 2010 Survey on CEO Succession Planning, conducted by Heidrick & Struggles and Rock Centre for Corporate Governance reveals some startling facts. Although their research is restricted to public and private firms in the U.S. and Canada, they offer valuable insights into succession planning:

- 69% of respondents thought that they needed a CEO successor to be "ready now", should the incumbent depart. Yet, only 54% were developing potential leaders to take on this role.

- 39% cited that they have "zero" viable internal candidates, which points out to a gap in people development and talent management.

- On an average, boards were found spend only 2 hours a year on CEO succession planning.

- Only half the companies surveyed had a written document elaborating the skills required for the next CEO.

- 71% of internal candidates knew they were in the formal talent development pool, but only 50% of them received regular communication. Communication gaps in these cases meant that prospective candidates who were not aware of being in the pipeline, could easily move out to other companies that offered attractive growth opportunities.

- 65% had not asked internal candidates whether the CEO role was acceptable to them. Many companies assume that internal candidates will always be ready to take on the CEO role. However, many top choices may refuse when actually offered the role, because of the spotlight and huge public scrutiny that surrounds the role.

- Only half the companies surveyed provided transition support for new CEOs.

Given the necessity of succession planning and the fact that most companies seem to avoid the process, because of the inherent difficulties, the issue draws all the more attention.

Towards Successful Succession Planning

Succession Planning and Management begins at the level of the CEO. From there, the company moves downward till it has covered the top and middle management, and may preferably reach out to the entire workforce. The first step to a structured Succession Plan is the creation of an interim Replacement Plan that has in place a back up to shoulder the responsibility of the organisation should the CEO suddenly depart.

Replacement Plan versus Succession Plan

A replacement plan is different from a succession plan in that it identifies the potential holders of a key position, but does not develop these resources to take on the role. Rather the incumbent in the role is considered to be a good model to train the potential candidate. However, succession planning objectively takes into account training needs and organizes the development of identified key people to nurture in them required competencies. While succession planning starts with a replacement plan, it must quickly be followed with a structured succession plan.

Building Blocks of a Successful Succession Plan

In order to serve its purpose, a succession plan must involve the following:

1. Identification and development of core competencies

2. Identification and development of potential key-position holders

3. A Succession Plan should also consider tying rewards and incentives to performance, so that key people who display the desired competencies and set performance benchmarks are appreciated and rewarded.

4. Succession planning is also tied to workforce planning. Workforce planning enables the review of job roles and identification of appropriate training needs, which are critical to the succession planning process.

A structured succession plan can be of two types:

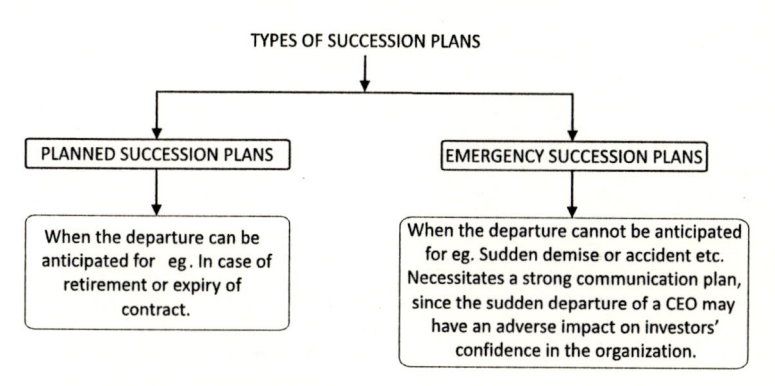

```
                    TYPES OF SUCCESSION PLANS
                              │
                ┌─────────────┴─────────────┐
                ▼                           ▼
    ┌───────────────────────┐   ┌───────────────────────┐
    │ PLANNED SUCCESSION    │   │ EMERGENCY SUCCESSION  │
    │ PLANS                 │   │ PLANS                 │
    └───────────┬───────────┘   └───────────┬───────────┘
                ▼                           ▼
    ┌───────────────────────┐   ┌───────────────────────────────┐
    │ When the departure    │   │ When the departure cannot be  │
    │ can be anticipated    │   │ anticipated for eg. Sudden    │
    │ for eg. In case of    │   │ demise or accident etc.       │
    │ retirement or expiry  │   │ Necessitates a strong         │
    │ of contract.          │   │ communication plan, since the │
    │                       │   │ sudden departure of a CEO may │
    │                       │   │ have an adverse impact on     │
    │                       │   │ investors' confidence in the  │
    │                       │   │ organization.                 │
    └───────────────────────┘   └───────────────────────────────┘
```

Figure 9.1 – Types of Succession Plans

1. Planned Succession plan: This is the case when departure of the CEO is anticipated due to retirement or contract expiry etc. Such a plan details the notice period a CEO must ensure, the incumbent CEO's role in the search for a successor, the "what" and "how" of knowledge transfer between the incumbent and the new CEO etc.

2. **Emergency Succession Plan:** An Emergency Succession Plan lays down the steps an organisation will take if the CEO or other key officials depart unexpectedly, due to an accident or death etc. Vital to an emergency succession plan is a detailed Communication Strategy, which indicates who will notify employees, stakeholders, and the media, and how the message will be delivered. In emergency departures, the feeling of loss is intense and often has implications on investor confidence in the firm. Thus, in addition to the other details that are included in a planned succession plan, an emergency succession plan necessitates a carefully drawn out communication plan.

THE BOARD AND THE CEO IN SPM

CEO Successions are substantial, important and inevitable changes that recur in the life of an organisation. Hence, given the high CEO turnover rates and accompanying business risks, succession planning has now become a high priority responsibility of the Board. While leaders may depart due to various reasons like underperformance, retirement etc., succession decisions are often difficult, and accompanied by corollaries regarding the existence of a suitable internal candidate or the need to replace other key executives appointed by the incumbent CEO. However, this transition can be made simpler, if there is considerable role clarity between the board and the CEO on how the process should be run.

Traditionally, companies assigned their Board of Directors the role of supervising the succession planning process, whereas the CEO was entrusted with the responsibility of conducting the entire process. However, due to certain inherent flaws in this system, publicly traded companies have now realized that an independent and objective Board is better placed to conduct the entire process and retain ownership over the same. Nevertheless, the importance of the CEO in managing succession planning remains paramount. In fact, to ensure effective management of this process, the roles and responsibilities of both the board and the CEO should be clearly defined and demarcated.

The Board and SPM

While succession planning is partnered by both the Board and the CEO, the onus lies majorly on the Board. Given its knowledge of business strategy and an objective viewpoint, the Board is considered better placed to guide the CEO in the succession process.

Broadly, the board's role can be summarized as follows:

1. Understand what the organisation needs to drive its strategy and culture.

2. Identify talents that may be targeted by rival organisations and retain them by offering a strong career path and growth opportunities.

3. Independently and objectively decide upon potential leadership holders.

4. Guide the CEO in developing this talent pool to take up leadership roles in future.

5. Spend adequate time on succession planning

6. Openly communicate with potential internal candidates, while simultaneously managing expectations to avoid circumstances of top contenders refusing to accept key roles when offered.

7. Supervise the succession planning process

While the Board guides the CEO through the process, the CEO's performance along this dimension could serve as a key performance indicator. Correspondingly, the Board must also take care to ensure an economic incentive for the incumbent CEO to motivate his engagement in the planning process.

For the Board and the CEO to operate in tandem towards a successful Succession Plan, both need to have a common understanding of the corporate strategy in terms of where the company is headed in the foreseeable future. Accordingly, consistent plans need to be drawn up.

While it may seem impossible for the CEO to maintain objectivity, the success of the planning process lies to a great extent on how diligently the CEO can follow Board guidelines, offering his perspectives and knowledge, wherever required, and how gracefully he can step aside to let the Board take the final call. However, if the CEO is much too attached to his status and cannot accept or prepare for a succession, the company may face a series of conflicts and power plays, ultimately disrupting work and order.

As far as selection of the new CEO is concerned, the Board needs to follow a comprehensive selection process: Many times, the Board may avoid a structured CEO selection process, preferring to rely on their instincts. An assessment process may be viewed as being too cumbersome or as limiting the freedom of the Board's judgement. Sometimes, the Board may avoid a structured selection process to avert possible offence to senior executives, who they believe, prefer not being assessed. However, CEO selection is a critical decision and must always follow a structured process because:

1. Comprehensive methods that run deeper than "experience" checks, to understand the prospective candidates' knowledge, skills, competencies and capabilities help take a more holistic decision.

2. While most potential candidates come with the required experience, decisions based exclusively on this can discount important factors such as personal attributes, mental orientation, willingness to learn, emotional adjustability, personality, work culture and values etc. These characteristics form an integral, unchangeable part of an individual and hence must be thoroughly assessed before arriving at a decision to ensure that the new CEO is a perfect fit in the organisation.

Some of the best practices for succession planning concluded through a research conducted by Oliver Wyman with the NACD:

- Discussions between the Board and the CEO regarding succession planning must ideally commence 3 to 5 years prior to the expected transition time.

- The entire Board must be part of the process.

- The CEO and the Board must engage in open and ongoing dialogue on succession planning, which should include a formal annual discussion of at least half a day.

- The CEO and the Board must have a common understanding on the company's strategic needs, and accordingly develop the criteria for CEO selection.

- The Board should employ formal assessment processes to judge candidates.

- Board members should interact with internal candidates in various settings.

- It is better to develop internal candidates than to opt for external recruitment.

- The outgoing CEO should either leave the Board immediately, or continue as Chairman for a period of 6 to 18 months.

- An emergency plan should be put in place and reviewed at least annually.

THE CEO AND SPM

Why is it so difficult for the CEO to remain objective when

it comes to succession planning? Precisely, because preparing his own successor to take charge of his area, is to accept the fact that eventually he must surrender the reigns to someone else. While this sounds quite natural, most of us human beings find it immensely difficult to accept this. Often, it builds a vacuum around the CEO, because by now, running the company or being in command has almost grown to be an integral part of his life, a way of life.

Often, the need to dominate can see CEOs and their executive teams get involved in power plays, the ultimate effect of which is detrimental to the organisation. Many times, they may delay the process of succession planning simply because they do not want to accept their imminent retirement. Sometimes, if there are strong personal relationships between the CEO and the Board members, the Board may also avoid discussions on the topic to avert anger, conflicts and outbursts. However, it is now that the Board must take on an active role to initiate the succession planning process before it is too late.

Thus, in the process of preparing the organisation for a succession, a fundamental quality that is desired of the incumbent CEO is that of a conscientious approach. Indeed, it takes an individual to transcend to a higher level of personal development to be able to place the good of the organisation above that of his own self. The brighter side here is that planning for his own succession would give the CEO more control over the process, and also in time, bring him the credit of being selfless and committed to the company, in the truest sense of the word.

The primary responsibility of the CEO therefore is to realize and accept the need for succession planning.

Secondly, the CEO can provide valuable insights on:

- Any gaps that exist between the company's work experience and skills and the desired core competencies.

- Prospective internal candidates, who can don the CEO role, should the company face an emergency.

From there, selection of the right person involves two important "transfers", which again is best executed by the incumbent CEO. These include: transfer of "vision" and transfer of "knowledge". Most often, the departure of a CEO can leave the company drifting aimlessly since the new CEO may not identify with the same vision that the old CEO held.

But, in a dynamic environment, losing direction is akin to suicide. Hence, good succession planning requires that the incumbent CEO spend quality time with potential successors to familiarize them with the vision, the status quo and the direction in which the company is headed. In addition, the CEO is responsible for developing potential successors, by imparting to them the knowledge and skill sets that the role demands. Often, the incumbent CEO is responsible for not only identifying and training prospective leaders for the CEO role, but also for mentoring them and creating in them an interest to step into the role.

The CEO's aid is also significant in the following:

- Creation of a Replacement Plan for direct reports, which may mean requesting a few individuals to temporarily accept additional responsibilities. The incumbent CEO, while embarking upon such a plan must be careful in treating job blocks. This is a situation where in a manager manning a key position is so indispensable for his role, that he cannot be promoted. In such a case, people who directly report to him are job blocked too.

- Initiating a Succession Plan for middle level managers.

- Creation of Succession Plans for all critical positions.

Thus, the CEO has an indispensable role to play in succession planning and his contribution to the process has significant bearing on how the company operates in future. It can practically make or mar the organisation's prospects. While there have been those who have avoided this exercise with grave results, Jeff Zelms is a particularly bright case I read of, of how a CEO can creatively and spectacularly leave his footprints behind.

In an attempt to identify the next CEO, Zelms, reigning CEO of Doe Run Corp., a MidWest mining and recycling organisation, initiated a five-person "Office of the President," comprising himself and four other key players. Together, the team began managing CEO duties and while Zelms used it as a smart tool to develop core competencies in his key people, he managed expectations regarding any decision on "the next CEO" by announcing that an external selection was always an option. Ultimately, after about a year and a half, one of the four key players, Bruce Neal, was identified as the best fit for the CEO role, and he succeeded Zelms in what seemed to be a relatively smooth transition. Subsequently, the company flourished, drawing upon the benefits that Zelms had initiated during his pre-retirement "Office of the President" days.

AND THEY LIVED HAPPILY EVER AFTER....

You have had a sturdy succession plan in place. Your outgoing CEO was the most cooperative one you have had in generations. The Board has selected the perfect candidate to take over as the new CEO. But does the process end there? No, you also need to ensure that you not only capitalise on the positive step but also also have plans in place "to live on happily ever after"...

The transition from an old CEO to a new one can often be a difficult time, not only for the employees and senior executives but also for investors and stakeholders. Every move, every gesture of the Board, the outgoing CEO and the new CEO now comes under the spotlight and carries implied meanings. The following "Things to remember" attempt to ease out the transition process:

- The Board needs to take important decisions regarding how to communicate the change to the employees as well as to the outgoing CEO, in order to smooth out transition – either by allowing the CEO to continue as Chairman or have him depart immediately and how to introduce the new CEO to the employee population and so on and so forth. Every gesture around this time quickly translates into an image that remains with the employees for years, often serving as signals of how they will be treated in future (more so in the case of a forced resignation or termination). Appropriate coaching and rehearsals are required to train both the incoming and outgoing executives on how to deliver in front of the audience, so as to leave a positive impact.

- Next, a detailed communication plan is needed to support the new executive in the first two to three months of his new term. Any change to the existing system, especially at a higher executive or leadership level is bound to create confusions and give rise to questions. Leaving these questions unanswered can create further chaos or disconnect. A well structured communication plan is a smart tool to manage this conundrum, if it can be published and send across to everyone within the first few days of change. The communication plan should briefly address questions regarding when the new CEO will come out with his vision statement or priorities, when will he intimate potential changes, whether he plans to undertake tours to various locations where the company has its offices and whether he plans to have individual or group meetings with specific departments etc. However, it should take care to provide concrete and specific inputs in terms of dates, events etc., so as to effectively erase doubt and confusion. Once approved by the new CEO, this document can be circulated to ensure a smooth leadership transition.

Considering that this communication plan is the new CEO's first substantial interaction with the employee population, and can serve as an important signal to the employees of his mode of operation, it needs to be carefully planned out. Also, it needs to be self explanatory, in the sense that it should take care not only to inform the public about his action plan, but also explain the reason behind his actions. Often, the CEO, may act from information unknown to the public and hence his actions may seem incongruent or incomprehensible to the employees, even when he acts from the best of intentions. Such a situation can trigger negative opinions if facts are left unexplained.

- While these strategies will help to ease the transition process from a leadership perspective, employees too need to prepare for the transition. Once they are aware of the mode of meetings expected (individual or group), employee representatives or team leads can be advised to ready themselves with a brief presentation on their respective areas – their current state of activities, recent achievements, key accountabilities, structure, future goals etc. This preliminary preparation sets the stage for meaningful discussion when the two parties interact, and ensures that maximum knowledge exchange takes place.

- While the new CEO can decide upon the mode of meetings, it is essential to begin with a few orientation meetings, which enable the incoming leader to interact directly with key teams and gain a perspective on their priorities and plans. Thus, an orientation strategy can always aid meaningful first communication plans between the key parties.

- In case the new CEO is an outsider, he will need to have a complete understanding of the historical background and context of the organisation, the company's evolution to its current level, any important events or turning points, the culture and norms etc. Thus, it is also important to plan out and organize fruitful meetings among the new CEO and senior executives who have served the company for a long time and are well aware of its history and culture.

- Finally, after the initial "getting to know you" phase, the Board needs to direct the CEO to prepare an assessment of the organisation, defining high priority areas that need immediate attention and a skeletal action plan to address the same. This can be taken as a framework to initiate strategic business discussions and lend to the company a defined direction, after the initial confusion of the transition process has passed over. Typically, the Board would require this analysis within three to six months of the transition.

CEO Succession remains one of the most difficult challenges in an organisation's lifecycle, and the better the succession planning process is the smoother the transition. Further, given that many well known organisations like Xerox, Apple and Dell have had successor CEO's underperform and replaced, to return power to the preceding CEO's, effective succession planning has assumed greater significance in recent times. The guidelines in this chapter are an attempt to help organisations effectively deal with this process and achieve transition with minimum friction.

CHAPTER 10 /

Able CEOs Leading The Organisational Change

*People don't resist change.
They resist being changed !*

~ *Peter Senge* ~

WHAT CAN WE LEARN FROM THEM?

Year 1981. A young entrepreneur ties up with friends to start a small software development firm. In 1992, 11 years later, surveys with prospective employees still show that a dismal 0% want to join the company.

A rough start, but can a company even think of making it big, of competing with established stallions in the industry if it cannot attract the right talent?

As it turns out, Narayana Murthy did. In fact, it was this heartbreaking revelation that led him to vow: "We will be number one in India in five years". Infosys grew leaps and bounds throughout the 1990's and in 1999, became the first Indian company to be listed in the Nasdaq Stock Market. By 2001, Infosys was one of the biggest software exporters from India, and the rest, as they say, is history.

With Narayana Murthy, it was sheer determination and perseverance, to begin with, which helped him engineer the change. From there, it was the zeal to do "new unusual things" that took him to the top. Murthy advocated creative thinking to turn out new ideas and think of new cost effective platforms to attract people. Indeed, Infosys scored heights by using a strong product, strong leadership, and sound business planning to their advantage.

Consider these Stories:

Year 2000. A large multinational company cuts a sorry figure at the bourses, as its stocks stumble, registering an ugly 30% dip in a day. The CEO, having issued three profit warnings in four months ultimately steps down, and is succeeded by a little known insider, Alan G. Lafley. Shares plunge further and the market was rife with speculation: Is the new CEO capable of achieving the level of change required?

Year 2004. A 70% growth in profits, whopping $51 billion revenue and a global market swept with new products, from home care to health care.

Five years and some sound change strategies was what it took Lafley to register a complete turnaround. Proctor & Gamble couldn't have witnessed a bigger change! Well almost...The celebrated Gillette acquisition was still to come!

Xerox too has an amazing transformation story.

When it set up its initial plain-paper copier in 1959, it was the first in the industry. For the next decade, it scaled echelons of growth, with revenues galloping from $60 million in 1961 to $500 million in 1965.

Crisis hit in the 1980's, when its market share slashed down by 50%, succumbing to tough Japanese competition, and the ROA fell to 8%.

The inflection came halfway through the 1980's, when it ramped up a major part of the market share back from the Japanese and registered an ROA of 14%. Paul Allaire took over as CEO of the company in 1990, and reorganized the entire corporate structure, also redefining the culture at work. In 1999, G. Richard Thoman succeeded as CEO, but unfortunately, his change efforts failed to produce the desired results, leading to Paul Allaire's comeback as CEO the next year. Xerox's turnaround is also largely attributable to Anne M. Mulcahy, who was appointed CEO in 2001. Today, with employee strength of about 130,000 employees, and the recent Affiliated Computer Services acquisition in February, 2010, Xerox remains one of the most trusted brands in the market.

What Xerox and P&G had in common was a dynamic

leadership that enabled them to rise every time they had a bad fall. In fact, there's a lot to learn from Alan Lafley, who calls himself "a serial change agent" for, often, in reviving a company, small, incremental changes turn out to be more beneficial than a radical change. And that is exactly what Alan did, till of course, the Gillette deal. Here are some thought processes that he used:

- When your people become mere players in the industry rather than winners, it's time to CHANGE! Lafley realized during his first 15 years with the company that often incremental business building reduces to a game, where targets are set, boundaries are pushed but just about enough to roll up the weakest competitor and gain a marginal high on share points. This leads to complacency, where just being in the game is considered as good as winning. Fact is it is not. Lafley argues that when the culture becomes such that being mere players becomes the acceptable norm, change calls for more than just romping up numbers-a cultural transformation. Sometimes though, change is a more obvious decision when you are up against strong, established competitors, as Lafley discovered when he was heading P&G's Asian operations with big names such as Nestle and Unilever as contenders.

- In initiating and pushing targets, however, Lafley recommends this: Always set "stretch" but realistic goals.

- Another practice that Lafley adopted was to define the "Core": core markets, brands, categories, technologies and capabilities. He realised that for a company as huge as P&G, operating over more than 100 countries, change could not touch all places at once. So, he identified 10 top priority countries that would be dealt with first. The lesson: handle change realistically.

- An even bigger learning to take from him is this: Clearly communicate the "core" to your people. It takes just one step more to tell them that "Our core businesses are a,b,c,d..", and once he'd done that, Lafley realized how people came up with questions regarding why their area was not a core area, what was required to turn it into a core, so leaders began to understand and vigorously participate.

- Lafley also put Kotter's repetition technique to use, going one step further to explain that employees, in general, are so cluttered with daily operational issues, that it is important to unclutter and have them soak in the "content" of change, make it a part of their system and then think in terms of how best to bring it around.

- Role Model. Even when they would miss earnings on two consecutive quarters, and profit pressure was tough, Lafley carried on with ambitious marketing plans, for their new brands that were up against established competitors, "to convince P&G managers we were going to go for winning."
- Another learning to take from Lafley is the need to clearly define what's going to change and what's not. Lafley, for instance, laid down what was not going to change – their purpose, value system and guiding principles. He went on to precisely define what he meant by each of those. So their purpose was to delight customers all over the world with P&G products of high quality, performance and value; their value system comprised integrity, trust, leadership and so on. Next, he defined what was going to change – businesses without a strategy would develop one, those that had strategies but were still not doing well would develop a new one, or plan better implementation of the existing one; and so on.
- Finally, he operated with the philosophy that the consumer rules. So, in any change initiative, the objective was to "delight" them with P&G products

  Another absolutely fantastic philosophy, that defined the thought process behind the Gillette deal, was this: "They're mechanical engineers. We're chemical engineers". Put them together and they can see lots of things that neither can individually. So, then you have new businesses that are born in the minds, and then materialized. The result: diversification, new products and new businesses.

- And there's one more thing. Lafley believes that his 25 years at P&G as operating manager gave him valuable insights into the dynamics of transforming the company. In steering change at the organisational level, deep knowledge of the company is essential, rather indispensable.

Xerox is an interesting maze of CEO decisions, and there's a lot to learn from its successes as well as its failures. A global document management company, it was established in 1906 as "The Haloid Photographic Company", before being renamed as "Xerox" in 1961. Having tested the market with an upgraded version of the prototype "Flat Plate", the company shot to fame in 1959, with Xerox 914 – the first plain paper copier machine. 914 became so popular that for a long time after that, Xerox enjoyed substantial revenue gains, introducing various product innovations and subsequently acquiring Scientific Data Systems in 1969. But easy gains made the company negligent to the fundamentals of their core business. In the mid 1980's, after losing substantial market share to their low cost Japanese competitors, the company's leadership used total quality techniques to revive manufacturing and customer service; and improve quality design and product alignment. Thus revitalized, Xerox became the first major U.S. Company to win back major market share from the Japanese.

In 1990, Paul Allaire took over as the CEO. One vantage point for Allaire was that he had been around in the company since 1966, having joined as a financial analyst, and had subsequently held various senior positions. Hence, he had a deep understanding of the organisation. Allaire introduced a series of changes, creating a new corporate structure, revising managerial roles and responsibilities, changing the selection and reward mechanism of managers, and revisiting the company's senior management ranks.

Soon, Allaire realized that Xerox depended too much on old fashioned analog copiers for its revenues, at a time when digital products were fast flooding the markets. He realized that in order to gain a competitive edge and secure a substantial revenue growth, they needed to shift focus from old fashioned analog copiers to digital technology. The subsequent development of digital photocopiers and Multi-Function Machines, that could be attached to computer networks earned Xerox a technical edge over its competitors. From there, Xerox laboured diligently to transform its product into a "service", coming up with a whole range of customer services - supply, maintenance, configuration and user support.

This was not an easy change though. When Allaire hired G. Richard Thoman as successor to his desk in 1997, he had hoped that Thoman would prove to be as successful a change agent in Xerox as he had been in IBM. Thoman took over as CEO of Xerox in 1999, with plans to shift to digital technology, cut costs, sell the company's financial services units and increase the number of retail outlets, among others. However, his efforts never worked out and led to a greater disaster, with the company reporting flat revenues in 1999.

It is said that, as a part of the transition process, Thoman had literally cannibalized the culture by converting Xerox's box salesman into consultants who sold systems. Thus, they were put through a process of unlearning and relearning that ripped them of their morale's. Ultimately, he stepped down after about a year, and Allaire returned as CEO. Why did Thoman, the brilliant change agent at IBM, fail so miserably with Xerox? There's a lot to learn from his moves, correct or otherwise:

1. Thoman successfully established "the burnt platform" kind of urgency, when he directed the strategic services department to cut a billion dollars in three years and went about cutting jobs wildly. It seems he also had a strategy in place that took care of his aspirations and objectives. Then what went wrong?

2. Even as he aggressively pursued change, Thoman, it turns out, did not show much concern for maintaining salespeople-customer relationships. Customers changed loyalties for rival products and this ultimately hit Xerox hard.

3. Thoman was perhaps so occupied with "achieving" the change that he hardly found time to communicate a clear vision to his people. Hence, while he was successful in establishing a sense of urgency, change efforts dissipated because people had no clear idea where Xerox was headed. Instead of cooperative, collaborative people efforts driving

the change, Thoman's efforts faced stiff opposition that crushed a successful turnaround.

In one of his statements, Thoman is said to have commented that, to certain degree, he was "deaf" to people concerns; since he feared that slowing down might mean never achieving the change. The underlying implication is that he was too aggressive and too fast for the change to sink in with the rest of the organisation. It could also hint that amidst the zeal to accomplish change, Thoman had assumed a possible reluctance to listen to his employee concerns. As indicated in an earlier chapter, employee concerns often point out important gaps in visioning and planning, and demand attention to minimize operational difficulties after the change has set in. Had Thoman made his people a part of his change attempts, rather than making them mere instruments of the change he had in mind, he might have made some very significant improvements to the organisation.

4. At a deeper level, Thoman's attempts may also have been influenced by Allaire who, a Business Week editorial claims, "continued to control the board of directors and sat in on key management meetings with Thoman, leaving

managers to wonder who was really in charge. Thoman, for his part, made a major blunder in not insisting on a free hand as CEO when he took over". While Allaire, during his term as CEO, had introduced and conceived significant changes for Xerox, this report would lead us to believe that he had nonetheless erred in not completely surrendering the reins to Thoman.

The Microsoft Transition from Bill Gates to Steve Ballmer

The anti-trust proceedings in the 1990s were a hard reality check for Microsoft. Although the final judgement was passed against an anticipated split in the company, it urged Bill Gates and Steve Ballmer to initiate Microsoft's gradual transition from an aggressive start up to a more mature organisation. As a start-up, Microsoft's culture was characterized by aggressiveness, competitiveness and a lack of discipline. In its early years after inception, from 1975 to 2000, Microsoft was largely run by Bill Gates, who took all decisions with respect to manpower, technology, marketing and sales, product planning etc.

However, in the 1980's, Gates had begun to realize that the entire burden of a slowly growing company was difficult for him to manage alone. Microsoft had grown leaps and bounds. Its revenues had increased from $3.79 billion in 1993 to $22.96 *billion in 2000, profits to $9.4 billion, and the headcount to 39,170. Between 1999 and 2000, the company hired nearly 8,000 new employees. Gates realized that he needed to devote more time to technology and shift focus from operational issues. In 2000, he appointed Steve Ballmer the CEO of Microsoft.*

The transition was not easy. Ballmer commented that neither he nor Gates understood the full implication of the power shift till they began exercising authority, and trying to figure out exactly which was whose domain. With time they began to understand their responsibilities better. Ballmer gradually assumed responsibility for setting the business vision and running the company in general, and while Gates continued to offer advice, major decisions regarding manpower planning, sales and marketing etc. were taken by Ballmer. Gates ruled as far as product development and technology decisions were concerned, but slowly drew him away from the other aspects of business. Ballmer decided to restructure the company's businesses, decentralizing segments and empowering their heads with the required resources in a bid to make them more independent, accountable and connected to customers. Slowly, Microsoft began to witness a shift in culture from being aggressive and competitive to open and respectful towards the external world. This marked Microsoft's gradual transition from the start up phase to a more mature organisation, a transition wherein both Gates and Ballmer had significant roles to play.

JACK WELCH: SPEED, SIMPLICITY, SELF CONFIDENCE

He wrote "The individual is the fountainhead of creativity and innovation, and we are struggling to get all of our people to accept the countercultural truth that often the best way to manage people is just to get out of their way. Only by releasing the energy and fire of our employees can we achieve the decisive, continuous productivity advantages that will give us the freedom to compete and win in any business anywhere on the globe."

Who is he?

He stepped down as CEO of General Electric in the year 2001, having taken the company from a market value of about $12 billion approximately $280 billion, in twenty years of committed leadership.

Jack Welch remains one of the most charismatic and magnetic personalities in corporate history. A legendary leader who transformed management and strategic thinking, Welch, CEO of General Electric from 1981 to 2001, almost made

GE synonymous with his own self. By the end of the 1980s, Welch's ideas on management came to be summarized by the motto "Speed, Simplicity, Self-Confidence".

Shortly after joining GE in 1960, Welch began to consider moving out to International Minerals & Chemicals, because he was disgusted with the marginal raise GE gave him and hated the company's rigid bureaucracy and red tapism. However, he stayed back, convinced by his superior, Reuben Gutoff, who had identified him as a key asset to the company. From there, he climbed the corporate ladder at lightning speed, serving several roles as Vice President, Senior Vice President and Chairman before becoming GE's youngest Chairman and CEO in 1981. In the twenty years that he reigned supreme, Welch took GE from a market value of $12 billion in 1981, to approximately $280 billion in 2001.

It's heartening to know more about the mind that steered an organisation through such phenomenal change; rather, Welch's was the mind that redefined change:

"Change in the marketplace isn't something to fear; it's an enormous opportunity to shuffle the deck, to replay the game.... Don't manage. Lead change before you have to.

When Jack Welch took over as CEO, GE was already between the maturity and decline phases of its life cycle. This implied that they were generating excess capacity in comparison to demand. To use this excess capacity, GE had started lowering prices, triggering a price war and reducing profit margins. Moreover, the company's organisation structure, resistance to change, bureaucracy, decision making process, information systems were all outmoded.

After assuming office as CEO, Welch traded obsolete businesses, selling those that had no potential future, for new ones that had the potential to top the industry. He retained only those businesses that were or had the scope to become number 1 or number 2 in their industry. Further, Welch modified the financial system and focused the organisation's capital to expand the capacity of these potential business units. Thus, under his leadership, GE made a strong comeback from the declining phase, somersaulting right back into the growth phase.

Welch pointed out that, in any great change, the starting point was always to paint a concrete picture of the future, and clearly define the purpose. From there, leaders were expected to inspire commitment towards the goal, to attain the desired objective.

In an interview with Harvard Business Review, Welch asserted, "Good business leaders create a vision, articulate the vision, passionately own the vision, and relentlessly drive it to completion."

He displayed tremendous leadership skills. He emphasized that to be a great leader; one must possess tons of energy and know how to use that fire to energize others. Welch laid a lot of stress on open communication between the leaders and the employees. By open, he meant straightforward and direct face to face interactions and conveying the whole truth. He was skilled at not only delivering messages, but ensuring that they stuck to the organisation's brains through persistent repetitions.

As CEO, Welch did away with the one thing that irked him most about GE in his initial days - the red tape and the bureaucracy. He introduced an informal learning environment, urging employees and executives to face reality, handle disagreement, and resolve conflicts through open argument. In a particularly hilarious account of this practice of constructive conflict, Robert M. Grant points out in his case study, how a GE executive once commented: "Jack will chase you around the room, throwing arguments and objections at you....Then you fight back until he lets you do what you want, and it's clear you'll do everything you can to make it work."

Welch was relentless with his employees. He is said to have fired the bottom 10% of his managers every year, inexorably pushing employees to perform. But, using the carrot and the stick method, he also rewarded the top 20% with bonuses and stock options. During his tenure, Welch expanded the stock options program at GE to include nearly one third of all employees and did all that was required to rip off the rigid hierarchy and promote informal learning, in a quest to drive progress.

In a beautiful, somewhat cubist take on stretch targets, Welch commented that to stretch, is to use dreams to set targets. You really don't know how you will achieve them when you set them. But eventually, you do end up measuring up to your target, and that, Welch says, is the time to set another stretch target. What a wonderful way of bringing Thoreau's thought *[It isn't wrong to build castles in the air. You just need to put a foundation beneath them.]* to life!

MICHAEL DELL: THE MIND THAT MADE DELL

Dell began as a modest venture by Michael Dell in the year

1984, when it was called PC's Limited. Since then Dell has had many substantial turning points, as when in 1986, Dell first ventured outside the US to Europe; or when their first stock offering took place in 1988 and so on and so forth. While Dell has seen phenomenal growth, it has also had its fair share of tumultuous changes. When Michael Dell returned as CEO after replacing CEO Kevin Rollins, Dell's PC brand had already fallen into second place behind HP. Its stock price had dipped 16 per cent from a year ago, and Dell, famous for double-digit sales growth had registered little success, with a negative unit growth of -11 percent in a certain quarter. Today, Dell is ranked 38 on the Fortune 500 (2010), and is also the fifth most admired company in its industry (Fortune 500 2010).

It is interesting to know the mind how Dell saw Dell through all of these changes.

Originating from Michael Dell's college business of building PCs with available parts, the company drew its leverage from a unique vantage point: the build-to-order strategy. This meant that Dell had a direct interface with the customers, having erased any middlemen, which in turn implied that he and his company could get a better hang of what clicked with the customer and what didn't. Further, having erased middlemen, Dell could also pass on savings to the customers in the form of lower costs. Also, Dell manufactured computers on customer requests. That meant there was practically zero wastage of resources in manufacturing a product which ran the risk of not being consumed. This implied cost cuts on staffing positions to move, manage and track inventory or rework systems that became obsolete before being purchased. This, along with a sharp sense of technological developments and a clear, strong customer focus helped Dell quickly transform his company into a leading multinational.

Yet, when Michael Dell went about investigating why Dell had cut a sorry growth relative to the industry, he found that they had focused on only one segment of their customers. While they were a hit with large companies and the government, they had completely neglected users in two other categories – individual consumers and small and medium businesses. An in depth analysis revealed that while 40 percent of the industry was composed of individual consumer and 37 percent of the industry comprised small and medium business, only 22 percent came from large companies and government.

So, while they had had good business with these relatively

stable, larger companies and had build up relationships that could last for decades (since they don't often change suppliers very frequently), that part of the market was only a meagre 22 percent. 78 percent of the market had gone unattended.

With changing markets and technological improvements in the external business environment, Dell realized that small and medium businesses were growing by leaps and bounds. Their customer base, as a result, was increasing and new requirements came in, even as users began going online for information and data that didn't exist before. This called for a re-visioning of their strategy, and Dell immediately set about identifying what was good and what was not about the way things worked. They identified new initiatives that could be integrated with their strategy to ensure maximum advantage out of competitive opportunities. They re-evaluated their product strategy and aligned it to develop products for small media business and introduced completely new product lines to cater to new groups of customers. So, in time, they had multiplied retail outlets across the world that sold Dell computers. They cut costs wherever possible to enable investment in areas that registered fast growth. At the same time, they realized that the organisation had to be quickly aligned with the revised strategy to obtain best results.

In what Michael Dell describes as "one of the more gut-wrenching" experiences, he had to do away with parts of the company that had begun to prove uncompetitive. While they took measures to handle the human aspect of these changes, by helping employees find suitable opportunities elsewhere, he identifies, that that was a necessary exercise to ensure the health of the organisation and restore stability.

Indeed Dell is a remarkable story of change and transformation. Change at Dell, seems natural with Michael Dell's rather unique attitude towards the six lettered menaces: "I think I've always approached my job by asking what the company needs to be successful. Whatever it is, I'm going to do it. And that means I have to change, "he says. In fact, to drive the message that change is important in order to progress and improve, Dell himself undertook the 360 degree feedback at an executive meeting, pointing out areas where he'd work on himself.

The world has produced many more leaders who like Welch, Lafley, Murthy, Dell, Gates and Ballmer continue to inspire us with their own transformational stories. Indeed they have all put to practice what John Schaar said –

"The future is not a result of choices among alternative paths offered by the present, but a place that is created — created first in the mind and will, create next in activity. The future is not some place we are going to, but one we are creating. The paths are not to be found, but made...."

CHAPTER 11 /
Conclusion

"Change is the main ingredient for Organisational Success"

~ *Percy Dastur* ~

UNDERSTANDING CHANGE MANAGEMENT

Given that change is as inevitable as it is difficult, the best way to manage change is to plan change initiatives in a holistic manner, so as to optimize the change results. Following a structured process, as shown in Chapter 2, helps keep a tab on the various issues related to a change initiative. In fact, it is important to follow a structured process because skipping steps only creates the illusion of speed and never produces a satisfying result.

Research indicates that Organisations transform either through drastic action or through evolutionary adaptation. Drastic action uses coercion to modify some aspect of the Organisation, in response to sudden changes in the external environment. Evolutionary adaptation is more gradual, decentralized, and produces an enduring effect with less turbulence.

The ideal way to ensure successful change results is through a mix of drastic action and evolutionary adaptation. Because traditional change programs typically involve drastic measures resulting in initiative overload, the employees react to change with strong resistance. The result is Organisational chaos. Eric Abrahamson, management professor at Columbia

Business School, suggests that "dynamic stability" is a better approach to managing change. This process consists of continuous but relatively small change efforts, that involve a reconfiguration of existing practices.

The principles of dynamic stability include tinkering, kludging, and pacing. Tinkering implies that companies should "toy" with the existing ideas, products, and policies that are currently in place. While tinkering may not guarantee a successful change, it is cost-effective and saves on time as compared to a process of "destruction and invention". Kludging implies tinkering at a higher management level and at a larger scale, thus throwing open possibilities of creation of new departments or businesses. Every company has a unique "change need" and "change speed". Pacing refers to the companies that have been transforming rapidly and need to shift down to tinkering and kludging.

UNDERSTANDING RESISTANCE TO CHANGE

The particular approach that a company adopts depends on its change need. But irrespective of the approach, one of the most important aspects of Organisational change from the change management point of view is "handling resistance to change". Resistance is the natural and invariable response to change, at least initially. It may be overt sometimes or hidden at other times, so identifying sources and types of resistance becomes a significant cue in handling the same.

In general, studies reveal that in an average Organisation, a change announcement is followed by a response structure as mentioned below:

- 15% of the workforce is eager to embrace it
- 15% of the workforce is absolutely against it
- 70% remain neutral, waiting to see what happens

It is important to understand that resistance can be managed only by working with people and dealing with their concerns.

Often people do not resist change. Rather they resist the transformation that the proposed change threatens to bring about in them. Many times, resistance to change is a form of defense mechanism caused by frustration and anxiety. Employees may well be able to recognize and understand the positive impact of change, but they nevertheless fret that once operational, the change might result in a loss of position, pay or influence. Rather than a consensus on the benefits from change, they nurse a collective fear regarding a potential unknown future, and their ability to adapt to it. For instance, a change to a new process or a new system of working may involve picking up new skills and technical expertise, whereas people may be apprehensive about their ability to develop or exercise these skills in the new work setting.

Sometimes, a change, although seemingly in the best interests of the Organisation, may be perceived as unfair by the employees. This in turn could lead to resentment among dissatisfied employees, often going to the extent of sabotage. Many times, the management shares a "personal relationship" with some employees, and when a change seems to threaten such "personal compacts", employees retaliate against it. Such disagreements involve mutual trust, loyalty and commitment and are hence deep rooted and difficult to uproot. An employee may hold commitments that are not in tandem with the change objective, and hence may respond negatively to change.

However, resistance to change is not always negative. In fact, many times probing resistance to change can enlighten even the top management about issues that otherwise skip notice. Employees who are likely to face the final impact of change may come up with insightful observations and well-intended disagreement that produces a more holistic understanding of the project at hand, as well as additional options and solutions.

MANAGING ORGANISATIONAL CHANGE

In order to glean the best out of any change effort, it is important, first, to get a top management or BOD approval on the project. This helps to ensure that the change goals are consistent with the overall company goals. The next step is to identify a champion who can voice the reasons behind and benefits from the change, in a manner that generates an Organisational buy-in to the change. Appropriate communication of the vision is of paramount significance. It is only when the vision is translated into a realistic plan that employee buy in is triggered. Communication also helps to educate the workforce on what, why and how of the proposed change. In its turn, this awareness creates an interest among people to involve and participate in the change. Also, companywide changes often warrant modifications in Organisational structures so as to sustain sweeping changes across the Organisation.

Things to Remember

COMMUNICATE: Organisational Changes are complex. Communication with the workforce regarding the potential need for change, the rationale behind the change, the Senior Management back up, the action plan etc. helps them understand the complexities and deal with the proposal in an informed manner.

INVOLVE: Involve people as much as possible, by encouraging them to talk out their concerns, so you know where the resistance might come from. Accordingly, you could either plan to deal with it at a higher level or put in place an employee team to manage the same.

SET CLEAR GOALS: Do not undertake a change for change sake. Have a clear objective in mind before embarking on a project and more importantly, communicate that goal to your people.

PLAN THE CHANGE: Once you have your goals clear, the next step is to plan what you will need to achieve that goal and what time frame you have at your disposal to achieve that change. Also focus on the coordination of different departments involved in the change, not on individual parts in isolation.

FOCUS, DELEGATE, MANAGE, CLOSE: Focus on meeting the needs of your customers and clients, both during and post the change. Try and delegate as much work as possible to your employees, empower and encourage them to take decisions. This helps build accountability and a sense of ownership, so employees feel responsible for driving the change. Understand and manage change, rather than trying to control it. Finally, celebrate your accomplishments.

ROLE OF PEOPLE FOCUSED CHANGE TEAMS

Transformation projects encompass multiple elements such as Business Processes, Systems, and most importantly, PEOPLE. When organizing the Change Project Team and extended project teams such as Business Representatives, Subject Matter Experts, etc., companies will always include the Functional Team, which covers the Business Processes, and the Technical Team, which focuses on the technology aspects of the project.

In addition, it is also important, that to manage the people side of change, an Organisation has in place a specialized

Organisational Change Management (OCM) Team. Several research studies have shown that 67 to 75 per cent of serious issues on change projects are due to people and change management issues, not software or technical problems. OCM initiatives provide visible results in handling this aspect of change. According to another study, 90% of the respondents, who included OCM initiatives in their projects rated the effect of OCM on project success as "very high" or "high".

Organisation wide changes involve modifications such as process changes, systems changes, Organisational structure changes, equipment changes, knowledge requirements changes, etc. OCM Teams are catered to manage the people side of change impact. Forming a change team is recommended for larger, more complex projects as well as for projects covering multiple functional areas, since the requirements, concerns, change readiness, and effects of change on the various stakeholder groups can be quite distinct. Forming a change team is also important for projects for which different stakeholders belong to different cultures or when multiple languages are involved.

The OCM Team should comprise a top level OCM Lead, the area Leads, and the extended OCM Team (which consists of

Change Agents). Where Organisations are not familiar with OCM, an OCM consultant is recommended to help them engineer the change process.

Organisation wide change is never a simple process. It is riddled with complexities and challenges, many of which become evident after the change process is set in motion. Many times, the change has to be stalled after an initial start due to other issues that become exigencies. Returning to these projects again then becomes a challenge in itself. Resistance, as we already said, is part of the package. Finance, Technology, Project Evaluation – every stage and every aspect requires able leadership to guide people through them. As the leader of the Organisation, the CEO plays a major role here, in not only communicating the change, but overseeing, coordinating and maintaining focus. Indeed, with the kind of authority, influence and credibility that the CEO wields, he remains an integral part of the entire Change Management Process.